WILLIAM SHAKESPEARE

HAMLET

The tragedy of Hamlet, Prince of Denmark

HAMBURGER LESEHEFTE VERLAG
HUSUM/NORDSEE

DRAMATIS PERSONAE

HAMLET, Prince of Denmark
CLAUDIUS, King of Denmark, Hamlet's uncle
The GHOST of the late king, Hamlet's father
GERTRUDE, the Queen, Hamlet's mother, now wife of Claudius
POLONIUS, councillor of State
LAERTES, Polonius's son
OPHELIA, Polonius's daughter
HORATIO, friend and confidant of Hamlet
ROSENCRANTZ,
GUILDENSTERN, } courtiers, former schoolfellows of Hamlet
FORTINBRAS, Prince of Norway
VOLTEMAND,
CORNELIUS, } Danish councillors, ambassadors to Norway
MARCELLUS,
BARNARDO,
FRANCISCO, } members of the King's Guard
OSRIC, a foppish courtier
REYNALDO, a servant of Polonius
Players
A Gentleman of the court
A Priest
A Grave-digger
The grave-digger's Companion
A Captain in Fortinbras's army
English Ambassadors
Lords, Ladies, Soldiers, Sailors, Messengers, and Attendants

SCENE. Elsinore: the Court and its environs.

ACT I

SCENE I

Enter Barnardo and Francisco, two Sentinels.

BARNARDO. Who's there?
FRANCISCO. Nay, answer me. Stand and unfold yourself.
BARNARDO. Long live the King!
FRANCISCO. Barnardo?
BARNARDO. He.
FRANCISCO. You come most carefully upon your hour.
BARNARDO. 'Tis now struck twelve. Get thee to bed, Francisco.
FRANCISCO. For this relief much thanks. 'Tis bitter cold,
And I am sick at heart.
BARNARDO. Have you had quiet guard?
FRANCISCO. Not a mouse stirring.
BARNARDO. Well, good night.
If you do meet Horatio and Marcellus,
The rivals of my watch, bid them make haste.
FRANCISCO. I think I hear them.
(Enter Horatio and Marcellus.)
Stand, ho! Who is there?
HORATIO. Friends to this ground.
MARCELLUS. And liegemen to the Dane.
FRANCISCO. Give you good night.
MARCELLUS. O, farewell honest soldier, who hath reliev'd you?
FRANCISCO. Barnardo hath my place. Give you good night.
(Exit.)
MARCELLUS. Holla, Barnardo!
BARNARDO. Say, what, is Horatio there?
HORATIO. A piece of him.
BARNARDO. Welcome, Horatio. Welcome, good Marcellus.
HORATIO. What, has this thing appear'd again tonight?
BARNARDO. I have seen nothing.
MARCELLUS. Horatio says 'tis but our fantasy,
And will not let belief take hold of him,
Touching this dreaded sight twice seen of us.
Therefore I have entreated him along
With us to watch the minutes of this night,
That if again this apparition come,
He may approve our eyes and speak to it.
HORATIO. Tush, tush, 'twill not appear.

BARNARDO. Sit down awhile,
And let us once again assail your ears,
That are so fortified against our story,
What we have two nights seen.
HORATIO. Well, sit we down.
And let us hear Barnardo speak of this.
BARNARDO. Last night of all,
When yond same star that's westward from the pole,
Had made his course t'illume that part of heaven
Where now it burns, Marcellus and myself,
The bell then beating one –
(Enter Ghost.)
MARCELLUS. Peace, break thee off. Look where it comes again.
BARNARDO. In the same figure like the King that's dead.
MARCELLUS. Thou art a scholar, speak to it, Horatio.
BARNARDO. Looks a not like the King? Mark it, Horatio.
HORATIO. Most like. It harrows me with fear and wonder.
BARNARDO. It would be spoke to.
MARCELLUS. Question it, Horatio.
HORATIO. What art thou that usurp'st this time of night,
Together with that fair and warlike form
In which the majesty of buried Denmark
Did sometimes march? By heaven, I charge thee speak.
MARCELLUS. It is offended.
BARNARDO. See, it stalks away.
HORATIO. Stay, speak, speak, I charge thee speak. *(Exit Ghost.)*
MARCELLUS. 'Tis gone and will not answer.
BARNARDO. How now, Horatio? You tremble and look pale.
Is not this something more than fantasy?
What think you on't?
HORATIO. Before my God, I might not this believe
Without the sensible and true avouch
Of mine own eyes.
MARCELLUS. Is it not like the King?
HORATIO. As thou art to thyself.
Such was the very armour he had on
When he th'ambitious Norway combated.
So frown'd he once, when in an angry parle
He smote the sledded Polacks on the ice.
'Tis strange.
MARCELLUS. Thus twice before, and jump at this dead hour,
With martial stalk hath he gone by our watch.
HORATIO. In what particular thought to work I know not,

But in the gross and scope of my opinion,
This bodes some strange eruption to our state.
MARCELLUS. Good now, sit down, and tell me, he that knows,
Why this same strict and most observant watch
So nightly toils the subject of the land,
And why such daily cast of brazen cannon
And foreign mart for implements of war,
Why such impress of shipwrights, whose sore task
Does not divide the Sunday from the week.
What might be toward that this sweaty haste
Doth make the night joint-labourer with the day,
Who is't that can inform me?
HORATIO. That can I.
At least the whisper goes so: our last King,
Whose image even but now appear'd to us,
Was as you know by Fortinbras of Norway,
Thereto prick'd on by a most emulate pride,
Dar'd to the combat; in which our valiant Hamlet
(For so this side of our known world esteem'd him)
Did slay this Fortinbras, who by a seal'd compact
Well ratified by law and heraldry
Did forfeit, with his life, all those his lands
Which he stood seiz'd of to the conqueror;
Against the which a moiety competent
Was gaged by our King, which had return'd
To the inheritance of Fortinbras,
Had he been vanquisher; as, by the same cov'nant
And carriage of the article design'd,
His fell to Hamlet. Now, sir, young Fortinbras,
Of unimproved mettle, hot and full,
Hath in the skirts of Norway here and there
Shark'd up a list of lawless resolutes
For food and diet to some enterprise
That hath a stomach in't, which is no other,
As it doth well appear unto our state,
But to recover of us by strong hand
And terms compulsatory those foresaid lands
So by his father lost. And this, I take it,
Is the main motive of our preparations,
The source of this our watch, and the chief head
Of this post-haste and rummage in the land.
BARNARDO. I think it be no other but e'en so.
Well may it sort that this portentous figure

Comes armed through our watch so like the King
That was and is the question of these wars.
HORATIO. A mote it is to trouble the mind's eye.
In the most high and palmy state of Rome,
A little ere the mightiest Julius fell,
The graves stood tenantless and the sheeted dead
Did squeak and gibber in the Roman streets;
As stars with trains of fire and dews of blood,
Disasters in the sun; and the moist star,
Upon whose influence Neptune's empire stands,
Was sick almost to doomsday with eclipse.
And even the like precurse of fear'd events,
As harbingers preceding still the fates
And prologue to the omen coming on,
Have heaven and earth together demonstrated
Unto our climatures and countrymen.
(Enter Ghost.)
But soft, behold. Lo, where it comes again.
I'll cross it though it blast me. *(Ghost spreads its arms.)*
Stay, illusion:
If thou hast any sound or use of voice,
Speak to me.
If there be any good thing to be done
That may to thee do ease, and grace to me,
Speak to me;
If thou art privy to thy country's fate,
Which, happily, foreknowing may avoid,
O speak;
Or if thou hast uphoarded in thy life
Extorted treasure in the womb of earth,
For which they say your spirits oft walk in death,
Speak of it, stay and speak. *(The cock crows.)*
Stop it, Marcellus.
MARCELLUS. Shall I strike at it with my partisan?
HORATIO. Do if it will not stand.
BARNARDO. 'Tis here.
HORATIO. 'Tis here. *(Exit Ghost.)*
MARCELLUS. 'Tis gone.
We do it wrong, being so majestical,
To offer it the show of violence,
For it is as the air, invulnerable,
And our vain blows malicious mockery.
BARNARDO. It was about to speak when the cock crew.

HORATIO. And then it started like a guilty thing
Upon a fearful summons. I have heard
The cock, that is the trumpet to the morn,
Doth with his lofty and shrill-sounding throat
Awake the god of day, and at his warning,
Whether in sea or fire, in earth or air,
Th'extravagant and erring spirit hies
To his confine; and of the truth herein
This present object made probation.
MARCELLUS. It faded on the crowing of the cock.
Some say that ever 'gainst that season comes
Wherein our Saviour's birth is celebrated,
This bird of dawning singeth all night long;
And then, they say, no spirit dare stir abroad,
The nights are wholesome, then no planets strike,
No fairy takes, nor witch hath power to charm,
So hallow'd and so gracious is that time.
HORATIO. So have I heard and do in part believe it.
But look, the morn in russet mantle clad
Walks o'er the dew of yon high eastward hill.
Break we our watch up, and by my advice
Let us impart what we have seen tonight
Unto young Hamlet; for upon my life
This spirit, dumb to us, will speak to him.
Do you consent we shall acquaint him with it
As needful in our loves, fitting our duty?
MARCELLUS. Let's do't, I pray, and I this morning know
Where we shall find him most convenient. *(Exeunt.)*

SCENE II

Flourish. Enter Claudius, King of Denmark, Gertrude the Queen, Council, including Voltemand, Cornelius, Polonius and his son Laertes, Hamlet, dressed in black, with Others.

KING. Though yet of Hamlet our dear brother's death
The memory be green, and that it us befitted
To bear our hearts in grief, and our whole kingdom
To be contracted in one brow of woe,
Yet so far hath discretion fought with nature
That we with wisest sorrow think on him

Together with remembrance of ourselves.
Therefore our sometime sister, now our queen,
Th'imperial jointress to this warlike state,
Have we, as 'twere with a defeated joy,
With an auspicious and a dropping eye,
With mirth in funeral and with dirge in marriage,
In equal scale weighing delight and dole,
Taken to wife. Nor have we herein barr'd
Your better wisdoms, which have freely gone
With this affair along. For all, our thanks.
Now follows that you know young Fortinbras,
Holding a weak supposal of our worth,
Or thinking by our late dear brother's death
Our state to be disjoint and out of frame,
Colleagued with this dream of his advantage,
He hath not fail'd to pester us with message
Importing the surrender of those lands
Lost by his father, with all bonds of law,
To our most valiant brother. So much for him.
Now for ourself, and for this time of meeting,
Thus much the business is: we have here writ
To Norway, uncle of young Fortinbras –
Who, impotent and bedrid, scarcely hears
Of this his nephew's purpose – to suppress
His further gait herein, in that the levies,
The lists, and full proportions are all made
Out of his subject; and we here dispatch
You, good Cornelius, and you, Voltemand,
For bearers of this greeting to old Norway,
Giving to you no further personal power
To business with the King more than the scope
Of these dilated articles allow.
Farewell, and let your haste commend your duty.

CORNELIUS AND VOLTEMAND.
In that, and all things, will we show our duty.

KING. We doubt it nothing. Heartily farewell.
(Exeunt Voltemand and Cornelius.)
And now, Laertes, what's the news with you?
You told us of some suit: what is't, Laertes?
You cannot speak of reason to the Dane
And lose your voice. What wouldst thou beg, Laertes,
That shall not be my offer, not thy asking?
The head is not more native to the heart,

The hand more instrumental to the mouth,
Than is the throne of Denmark to thy father.
What wouldst thou have, Laertes?
LAERTES. My dread lord,
Your leave and favour to return to France,
From whence though willingly I came to Denmark
To show my duty in your coronation,
Yet now I must confess, that duty done,
My thoughts and wishes bend again toward France
And bow them to your gracious leave and pardon.
KING. Have you your father's leave? What says Polonius?
POLONIUS. He hath, my lord, wrung from me my slow leave
By laboursome petition, and at last
Upon his will I seal'd my hard consent.
I do beseech you give him leave to go.
KING. Take thy fair hour, Laertes, time be thine,
And thy best graces spend it at thy will.
But now, my cousin Hamlet, and my son –
HAMLET. A little more than kin, and less than kind.
KING. How is it that the clouds still hang on you?
HAMLET. Not so, my lord, I am too much in the sun.
QUEEN. Good Hamlet, cast thy nighted colour off,
And let thine eye look like a friend on Denmark.
Do not for ever with thy vailed lids
Seek for thy noble father in the dust.
Thou know'st 'tis common: all that lives must die,
Passing through nature to eternity.
HAMLET. Ay, madam, it is common.
QUEEN. If it be,
Why seems it so particular with thee?
HAMLET. Seems, madam? Nay, it is. I know not "seems".
'Tis not alone my inky cloak, good mother,
Nor customary suits of solemn black,
Nor windy suspiration of forc'd breath,
No, nor the fruitful river in the eye,
Nor the dejected haviour of the visage,
Together with all forms, moods, shapes of grief,
That can denote me truly. These indeed seem,
For they are actions that a man might play;
But I have that within which passes show,
These but the trappings and the suits of woe.
KING. 'Tis sweet and commendable in your nature, Hamlet,
To give these mourning duties to your father,

But you must know your father lost a father,
That father lost, lost his – and the survivor bound
In filial obligation for some term
To do obsequious sorrow. But to persever
In obstinate condolement is a course
Of impious stubbornness, 'tis unmanly grief,
It shows a will most incorrect to heaven,
A heart unfortified, a mind impatient,
An understanding simple and unschool'd;
For what we know must be, and is as common
As any the most vulgar thing to sense –
Why should we in our peevish opposition
Take it to heart? Fie, 'tis a fault to heaven,
A fault against the dead, a fault to nature,
To reason most absurd, whose common theme
Is death of fathers, and who still hath cried
From the first corse till he that died today,
"This must be so". We pray you throw to earth
This unprevailing woe, and think of us
As of a father; for let the world take note
You are the most immediate to our throne,
And with no less nobility of love
Than that which dearest father bears his son
Do I impart toward you. For your intent
In going back to school in Wittenberg,
It is most retrograde to our desire,
And we beseech you bend you to remain
Here in the cheer and comfort of our eye,
Our chiefest courtier, cousin, and our son.
QUEEN. Let not thy mother lose her prayers, Hamlet.
I pray thee stay with us, go not to Wittenberg.
HAMLET. I shall in all my best obey you, madam.
KING. Why, 'tis a loving and a fair reply.
Be as ourself in Denmark. Madam, come.
This gentle and unforc'd accord of Hamlet
Sits smiling to my heart; in grace whereof
No jocund health that Denmark drinks today
But the great cannon to the clouds shall tell,
And the King's rouse the heaven shall bruit again,
Re-speaking earthly thunder. Come away.
(Flourish. Exeunt all but Hamlet.)
HAMLET. O that this too too sullied flesh would melt,
Thaw and resolve itself into a dew,

Or that the Everlasting had not fix'd
His canon 'gainst self-slaughter. O God! God!
How weary, stale, flat, and unprofitable
Seem to me all the uses of this world!
Fie on't, ah fie, 'tis an unweeded garden
That grows to seed; things rank and gross in nature
Possess it merely. That it should come to this!
But two months dead – nay, not so much, not two –
So excellent a king, that was to this
Hyperion to a satyr, so loving to my mother
That he might not beteem the winds of heaven
Visit her face too roughly. Heaven and earth,
Must I remember? Why, she would hang on him
As if increase of appetite had grown
By what it fed on; and yet within a month –
Let me not think on't – Frailty, thy name is woman –
A little month, or ere those shoes were old
With which she follow'd my poor father's body,
Like Niobe, all tears – why, she –
O God, a beast that wants discourse of reason
Would have mourn'd longer – married with my uncle,
My father's brother – but no more like my father
Than I to Hercules. Within a month,
Ere yet the salt of most unrighteous tears
Had left the flushing in her galled eyes,
She married – O most wicked speed! To post
With such dexterity to incestuous sheets!
It is not, nor it cannot come to good.
But break, my heart, for I must hold my tongue.

(Enter Horatio, Marcellus, and Barnardo.)

HORATIO. Hail to your lordship.
HAMLET. I am glad to see you well.
Horatio, or I do forget myself.
HORATIO. The same, my lord, and your poor servant ever.
HAMLET. Sir, my good friend, I'll change that name with you.
And what make you from Wittenberg, Horatio? –
Marcellus.
MARCELLUS. My good lord.
HAMLET.
I am very glad to see you. – *(To Barnardo)* Good even sir. –
But what in faith make you from Wittenberg?
HORATIO. A truant disposition, good my lord.
HAMLET. I would not hear your enemy say so,

Nor shall you do my ear that violence
To make it truster of your own report
Against yourself. I know you are no truant.
But what is your affair in Elsinore?
We'll teach you to drink deep ere you depart.
HORATIO. My lord, I came to see your father's funeral.
HAMLET. I prithee do not mock me, fellow-student.
I think it was to see my mother's wedding.
HORATIO. Indeed, my lord, it follow'd hard upon.
HAMLET. Thrift, thrift, Horatio. The funeral bak'd meats
Did coldly furnish forth the marriage tables.
Would I had met my dearest foe in heaven
Or ever I had seen that day, Horatio.
My father – methinks I see my father –
HORATIO. Where, my lord?
HAMLET. In my mind's eye, Horatio.
HORATIO. I saw him once; a was a goodly king.
HAMLET. A was a man, take him for all in all:
I shall not look upon his like again.
HORATIO. My lord, I think I saw him yesternight.
HAMLET. Saw? Who?
HORATIO. My lord, the king your father.
HAMLET. The king my father?
HORATIO. Season your admiration for a while
With an attent ear till I may deliver
Upon the witness of these gentlemen
This marvel to you.
HAMLET. For God's love let me hear!
HORATIO. Two nights together had these gentlemen,
Marcellus and Barnardo, on their watch
In the dead waste and middle of the night
Been thus encounter'd: a figure like your father
Armed at point exactly, cap-à-pie,
Appears before them, and with solemn march
Goes slow and stately by them; thrice he walk'd
By their oppress'd and fear-surprised eyes
Within his truncheon's length, whilst they, distill'd
Almost to jelly with the act of fear,
Stand dumb and speak not to him. This to me
In dreadful secrecy impart they did,
And I with them the third night kept the watch,
Where, as they had deliver'd, both in time,
Form of the thing, each word made true and good,

The apparition comes. I knew your father;
These hands are not more like.
HAMLET. But where was this?
MARCELLUS. My lord, upon the platform where we watch.
HAMLET. Did you not speak to it?
HORATIO. My lord, I did,
But answer made it none. Yet once methought
It lifted up it head and did address
Itself to motion like as it would speak.
But even then the morning cock crew loud,
And at the sound it shrunk in haste away
And vanish'd from our sight.
HAMLET. 'Tis very strange.
HORATIO. As I do live, my honour'd lord, 'tis true;
And we did think it writ down in our duty
To let you know of it.
HAMLET. Indeed, sirs; but this troubles me.
Hold you the watch tonight?
ALL. We do, my lord.
HAMLET. Arm'd, say you?
ALL. Arm'd, my lord.
HAMLET. From top to toe?
ALL. My lord, from head to foot.
HAMLET. Then saw you not his face?
HORATIO. O yes, my lord, he wore his beaver up.
HAMLET. What look'd he, frowningly?
HORATIO. A countenance more in sorrow than in anger.
HAMLET. Pale, or red?
HORATIO. Nay, very pale.
HAMLET. And fix'd his eyes upon you?
HORATIO. Most constantly.
HAMLET. I would I had been there.
HORATIO. It would have much amaz'd you.
HAMLET. Very like.
Stay'd it long?
HORATIO. While one with moderate haste might tell a hundred.
MARCELLUS AND BARNARDO. Longer, longer.
HORATIO. Not when I saw't.
HAMLET. His beard was grizzled, no?
HORATIO. It was as I have seen it in his life,
A sable silver'd.
HAMLET. I will watch tonight.
Perchance 'twill walk again.

HORATIO. I war'nt it will.
HAMLET. If it assume my noble father's person,
I'll speak to it though hell itself should gape
And bid me hold my peace. I pray you all,
If you have hitherto conceal'd this sight,
Let it be tenable in your silence still;
And whatsomever else shall hap tonight,
Give it an understanding but no tongue.
I will requite your loves. So fare you well.
Upon the platform 'twixt eleven and twelve
I'll visit you.
ALL. Our duty to your honour.
HAMLET. Your loves, as mine to you. Farewell.
(Exeunt Horatio, Marcellus, and Barnardo.)
My father's spirit – in arms! All is not well.
I doubt some foul play. Would the night were come.
Till then sit still, my soul. Foul deeds will rise,
Though all the earth o'erwhelm them, to men's eyes.
(Exit.)

SCENE III

Enter Laertes and Ophelia, his sister.

LAERTES. My necessaries are embark'd. Farewell.
And sister, as the winds give benefit
And convoy is assistant, do not sleep,
But let me hear from you.
OPHELIA. Do you doubt that?
LAERTES. For Hamlet, and the trifling of his favour,
Hold it a fashion and a toy in blood,
A violet in the youth of primy nature,
Forward, not permanent, sweet, not lasting,
The perfume and suppliance of a minute,
No more.
OPHELIA. No more but so?
LAERTES. Think it no more.
For nature crescent does not grow alone
In thews and bulk, but as this temple waxes,
The inward service of the mind and soul
Grows wide withal. Perhaps he loves you now,
And now no soil nor cautel doth besmirch

The virtue of his will; but you must fear,
His greatness weigh'd, his will is not his own.
For he himself is subject to his birth:
He may not, as unvalu'd persons do,
Carve for himself, for on his choice depends
The sanity and health of this whole state;
And therefore must his choice be circumscrib'd
Unto the voice and yielding of that body
Whereof he is the head. Then if he says he loves you,
It fits your wisdom so far to believe it
As he in his particular act and place
May give his saying deed; which is no further
Than the main voice of Denmark goes withal.
Then weigh what loss your honour may sustain
If with too credent ear you list his songs,
Or lose your heart, or your chaste treasure open
To his unmaster'd importunity.
Fear it, Ophelia, fear it, my dear sister,
And keep you in the rear of your affection
Out of the shot and danger of desire.
The chariest maid is prodigal enough
If she unmask her beauty to the moon.
Virtue itself scapes not calumnious strokes.
The canker galls the infants of the spring
Too oft before their buttons be disclos'd,
And in the morn and liquid dew of youth
Contagious blastments are most imminent.
Be wary then: best safety lies in fear.
Youth to itself rebels, though none else near.

OPHELIA. I shall th'effect of this good lesson keep
As watchman to my heart. But good my brother,
Do not as some ungracious pastors do,
Show me the steep and thorny way to heaven,
Whiles like a puff'd and reckless libertine
Himself the primrose path of dalliance treads,
And recks not his own rede.

LAERTES. O fear me not.
I stay too long.

(Enter Polonius.)

But here my father comes.
A double blessing is a double grace:
Occasion smiles upon a second leave.

POLONIUS. Yet here, Laertes? Aboard, aboard for shame.

The wind sits in the shoulder of your sail,
And you are stay'd for. There, my blessing with thee.
And these few precepts in thy memory
Look thou character. Give thy thoughts no tongue,
Nor any unproportion'd thought his act.
Be thou familiar, but by no means vulgar;
Those friends thou hast, and their adoption tried,
Grapple them unto thy soul with hoops of steel,
But do not dull thy palm with entertainment
Of each new-hatch'd, unfledg'd courage. Beware
Of entrance to a quarrel, but being in,
Bear't that th'opposed may beware of thee.
Give every man thy ear, but few thy voice;
Take each man's censure, but reserve thy judgment.
Costly thy habit as thy purse can buy,
But not express'd in fancy; rich, not gaudy;
For the apparel oft proclaims the man,
And they in France of the best rank and station
Are of a most select and generous chief in that.
Neither a borrower nor a lender be,
For loan oft loses both itself and friend,
And borrowing dulls the edge of husbandry.
This above all: to thine own self be true,
And it must follow as the night the day
Thou canst not then be false to any man.
Farewell, my blessing season this in thee.
LAERTES. Most humbly do I take my leave, my lord.
POLONIUS. The time invests you; go, your servants tend.
LAERTES. Farewell, Ophelia, and remember well
What I have said to you.
OPHELIA. 'Tis in my memory lock'd,
And you yourself shall keep the key of it.
LAERTES. Farewell. *(Exit.)*
POLONIUS. What is't, Ophelia, he hath said to you?
OPHELIA. So please you, something touching the Lord Hamlet.
POLONIUS. Marry, well bethought.
'Tis told me he hath very oft of late
Given private time to you, and you yourself
Have of your audience been most free and bounteous.
If it be so – as so 'tis put on me,
And that in way of caution – I must tell you
You do not understand yourself so clearly
As it behoves my daughter and your honour.

What is between you? Give me up the truth.
OPHELIA. He hath, my lord, of late made many tenders
Of his affection to me.
POLONIUS. Affection? Pooh, you speak like a green girl,
Unsifted in such perilous circumstance.
Do you believe his tenders, as you call them?
OPHELIA. I do not know, my lord, what I should think.
POLONIUS. Marry, I will teach you. Think yourself a baby
That you have ta'en these tenders for true pay
Which are not sterling. Tender yourself more dearly
Or – not to crack the wind of the poor phrase,
Running it thus – you'll tender me a fool.
OPHELIA. My lord, he hath importun'd me with love
In honourable fashion.
POLONIUS. Ay, fashion you may call it. Go to, go to.
OPHELIA. And hath given countenance to his speech, my lord,
With almost all the holy vows of heaven.
POLONIUS. Ay, springes to catch woodcocks. I do know,
When the blood burns, how prodigal the soul
Lends the tongue vows. These blazes, daughter,
Giving more light than heat, extinct in both
Even in their promise as it is a-making,
You must not take for fire. From this time
Be something scanter of your maiden presence,
Set your entreatments at a higher rate
Than a command to parley. For Lord Hamlet,
Believe so much in him that he is young,
And with a larger tether may he walk
Than may be given you. In few, Ophelia,
Do not believe his vows; for they are brokers
Not of that dye which their investments show,
But mere implorators of unholy suits,
Breathing like sanctified and pious bawds
The better to beguile. This is for all.
I would not, in plain terms, from this time forth
Have you so slander any moment leisure
As to give words or talk with the Lord Hamlet.
Look to't, I charge you. Come your ways.
OPHELIA. I shall obey, my lord.

(Exeunt.)

SCENE IV

Enter Hamlet, Horatio, and Marcellus.

HAMLET. The air bites shrewdly, it is very cold.
HORATIO. It is a nipping and an eager air.
HAMLET. What hour now?
HORATIO. I think it lacks of twelve.
MARCELLUS. No, it is struck.
HORATIO. Indeed? I heard it not.
It then draws near the season
Wherein the spirit held his wont to walk.
(A flourish of trumpets, and two pieces of ordnance go off.)
What does this mean, my lord?
HAMLET. The King doth wake tonight and takes his rouse,
Keeps wassail, and the swagg'ring upspring reels;
And as he drains his draughts of Rhenish down,
The kettle-drum and trumpet thus bray out
The triumph of his pledge.
HORATIO. Is it a custom?
HAMLET. Ay marry is't,
But to my mind, though I am native here
And to the manner born, it is a custom
More honour'd in the breach than the observance.
This heavy-headed revel east and west
Makes us traduc'd and tax'd of other nations –
They clepe us drunkards, and with swinish phrase
Soil our addition; and indeed it takes
From our achievements, though perform'd at height,
The pith and marrow of our attribute.
So, oft it chances in particular men
That for some vicious mole of nature in them,
As in their birth, wherein they are not guilty
(Since nature cannot choose his origin),
By their o'ergrowth of some complexion,
Oft breaking down the pales and forts of reason,
Or by some habit, that too much o'erleavens
The form of plausive manners – that these men,
Carrying, I say, the stamp of one defect,
Being Nature's livery or Fortune's star,
His virtues else, be they as pure as grace,
As infinite as man may undergo,
Shall in the general censure take corruption

From that particular fault. The dram of evil
Doth all the noble substance often dout
To his own scandal.

(Enter Ghost.)

HORATIO. Look, my lord, it comes.

HAMLET. Angels and ministers of grace defend us!
Be thou a spirit of health or goblin damn'd,
Bring with thee airs from heaven or blasts from hell,
Be thy intents wicked or charitable,
Thou com'st in such a questionable shape
That I will speak to thee. I'll call thee Hamlet,
King, father, royal Dane. O answer me.
Let me not burst in ignorance, but tell
Why thy canoniz'd bones, hearsed in death,
Have burst their cerements, why the sepulchre
Wherein we saw thee quietly inurn'd
Hath op'd his ponderous and marble jaws
To cast thee up again. What may this mean,
That thou, dead corse, again in complete steel
Revisits thus the glimpses of the moon,
Making night hideous and we fools of nature
So horridly to shake our disposition
With thoughts beyond the reaches of our souls?
Say why is this? Wherefore? What should we do?

(Ghost beckons.)

HORATIO. It beckons you to go away with it,
As if it some impartment did desire
To you alone.

MARCELLUS. Look with what courteous action
It waves you to a more removed ground.
But do not go with it.

HORATIO. No, by no means.

HAMLET. It will not speak. Then I will follow it.

HORATIO. Do not, my lord.

HAMLET. Why, what should be the fear?
I do not set my life at a pin's fee,
And for my soul, what can it do to that,
Being a thing immortal as itself?
It waves me forth again. I'll follow it.

HORATIO. What if it tempt you toward the flood, my lord,
Or to the dreadful summit of the cliff
That beetles o'er his base into the sea,
And there assume some other horrible form

Which might deprive your sovereignty of reason
And draw you into madness? Think of it.
The very place puts toys of desperation,
Without more motive, into every brain
That looks so many fathoms to the sea
And hears it roar beneath.

HAMLET. It waves me still.
Go on, I'll follow thee.

MARCELLUS. You shall not go, my lord.

HAMLET. Hold off your hands.

HORATIO. Be rul'd; you shall not go.

HAMLET. My fate cries out
And makes each petty artire in this body
As hardy as the Nemean lion's nerve.
Still am I call'd. Unhand me, gentlemen.
By heaven, I'll make a ghost of him that lets me.
I say away. – Go on, I'll follow thee.

(Exeunt Ghost and Hamlet.)

HORATIO. He waxes desperate with imagination.

MARCELLUS. Let's follow. 'Tis not fit thus to obey him.

HORATIO. Have after. To what issue will this come?

MARCELLUS. Something is rotten in the state of Denmark.

HORATIO. Heaven will direct it.

MARCELLUS. Nay, let's follow him.

(Exeunt.)

SCENE V

Enter Ghost and Hamlet.

HAMLET. Whither wilt thou lead me? Speak, I'll go no further.

GHOST. Mark me.

HAMLET. I will.

GHOST. My hour is almost come
When I to sulph'rous and tormenting flames
Must render up myself.

HAMLET. Alas, poor ghost.

GHOST. Pity me not, but lend thy serious hearing
To what I shall unfold.

HAMLET. Speak, I am bound to hear.

GHOST. So art thou to revenge when thou shalt hear.

HAMLET. What?

GHOST. I am thy father's spirit,
Doom'd for a certain term to walk the night,
And for the day confin'd to fast in fires,
Till the foul crimes done in my days of nature
Are burnt and purg'd away. But that I am forbid
To tell the secrets of my prison-house,
I could a tale unfold whose lightest word
Would harrow up thy soul, freeze thy young blood,
Make thy two eyes like stars start from their spheres,
Thy knotted and combined locks to part,
And each particular hair to stand an end
Like quills upon the fretful porpentine.
But this eternal blazon must not be
To ears of flesh and blood. List, list, O list!
If thou didst ever thy dear father love –
HAMLET. O God!
GHOST. Revenge his foul and most unnatural murder.
HAMLET. Murder!
GHOST. Murder most foul, as in the best it is,
But this most foul, strange and unnatural.
HAMLET. Haste me to know't, that I with wings as swift
As meditation or the thoughts of love
May sweep to my revenge.
GHOST. I find thee apt.
And duller shouldst thou be than the fat weed
That roots itself in ease on Lethe wharf,
Wouldst thou not stir in this. Now, Hamlet, hear.
'Tis given out that, sleeping in my orchard,
A serpent stung me – so the whole ear of Denmark
Is by a forged process of my death
Rankly abus'd – but know, thou noble youth,
The serpent that did sting thy father's life
Now wears his crown.
HAMLET. O my prophetic soul! My uncle!
GHOST. Ay, that incestuous, that adulterate beast,
With witchcraft of his wit, with traitorous gifts –
O wicked wit, and gifts that have the power
So to seduce! – won to his shameful lust
The will of my most seeming-virtuous queen.
O Hamlet, what a falling off was there,
From me, whose love was of that dignity
That it went hand in hand even with the vow
I made to her in marriage, and to decline

Upon a wretch whose natural gifts were poor
To those of mine.
But virtue, as it never will be mov'd,
Though lewdness court it in a shape of heaven,
So lust, though to a radiant angel link'd,
Will sate itself in a celestial bed
And prey on garbage.
But soft, methinks I scent the morning air:
Brief let me be. Sleeping within my orchard,
My custom always of the afternoon,
Upon my secure hour thy uncle stole
With juice of cursed hebenon in a vial,
And in the porches of my ears did pour
The leperous distilment, whose effect
Holds such an enmity with blood of man
That swift as quicksilver it courses through
The natural gates and alleys of the body,
And with a sudden vigour it doth posset
And curd, like eager droppings into milk,
The thin and wholesome blood. So did it mine,
And a most instant tetter bark'd about,
Most lazar-like, with vile and loathsome crust
All my smooth body.
Thus was I, sleeping, by a brother's hand
Of life, of crown, of queen at once dispatch'd,
Cut off even in the blossoms of my sin,
Unhousel'd, disappointed, unanel'd,
No reck'ning made, but sent to my account
With all my imperfections on my head.
O horrible! O horrible! most horrible!
If thou has nature in thee, bear it not,
Let not the royal bed of Denmark be
A couch for luxury and damned incest.
But howsomever thou pursuest this act,
Taint not thy mind nor let thy soul contrive
Against thy mother aught. Leave her to heaven,
And to those thorns that in her bosom lodge
To prick and sting her. Fare thee well at once:
The glow-worm shows the matin to be near
And gins to pale his uneffectual fire.
Adieu, adieu, adieu. Remember me. *(Exit.)*
HAMLET. O all you host of heaven! O earth! What else?
And shall I couple hell? O fie! Hold, hold, my heart,

And you, my sinews, grow not instant old,
But bear me stiffly up. Remember thee?
Ay, thou poor ghost, whiles memory holds a seat
In this distracted globe. Remember thee?
Yea, from the table of my memory
I'll wipe away all trivial fond records,
All saws of books, all forms, all pressures past
That youth and observation copied there,
And thy commandment all alone shall live
Within the book and volume of my brain,
Unmix'd with baser matter. Yes, by heaven!
O most pernicious woman!
O villain, villain, smiling damned villain!
My tables. Meet it is I set it down
That one may smile, and smile, and be a villain –
At least I am sure it may be so in Denmark. *(Writes.)*
So, uncle, there you are. Now to my word.
It is "Adieu, adieu, remember me."
I have sworn't.

(Enter Horatio and Marcellus, calling.)

HORATIO. My lord, my lord.
MARCELLUS. Lord Hamlet.
HORATIO. Heavens secure him.
HAMLET *(aside)*. So be it.
MARCELLUS. Hillo, ho, ho, my lord.
HAMLET. Hillo, ho, ho, boy. Come, bird, come.
MARCELLUS. How is't, my noble lord?
HORATIO. What news, my lord?
HAMLET. O, wonderful!
HORATIO. Good my lord, tell it.
HAMLET. No, you will reveal it.
HORATIO. Not I, my lord, by heaven.
MARCELLUS. Nor I, my lord.
HAMLET. How say you then, would heart of man once think it –
But you'll be secret?
HORATIO AND MARCELLUS. Ay, by heaven.
HAMLET. There's never a villain dwelling in all Denmark
But he's an arrant knave.
HORATIO. There needs no ghost, my lord, come from the grave
To tell us this.
HAMLET. Why, right, you are in the right.
And so without more circumstance at all
I hold it fit that we shake hands and part,

You as your business and desire shall point you –
For every man hath business and desire,
Such as it is – and for my own poor part,
I will go pray.
HORATIO. These are but wild and whirling words, my lord.
HAMLET. I am sorry they offend you, heartily –
Yes faith, heartily.
HORATIO. There's no offence, my lord.
HAMLET. Yes by Saint Patrick but there is, Horatio,
And much offence too. Touching this vision here,
It is an honest ghost, that let me tell you.
For your desire to know what is between us,
O'ermaster't as you may. And now, good friends,
As you are friends, scholars, and soldiers,
Give me one poor request.
HORATIO. What is't, my lord? We will.
HAMLET. Never make known what you have seen tonight.
HORATIO AND MARCELLUS. My lord, we will not.
HAMLET. Nay, but swear't.
HORATIO. In faith, my lord, not I.
MARCELLUS. Nor I, my lord, in faith.
HAMLET. Upon my sword.
MARCELLUS. We have sworn, my lord, already.
HAMLET. Indeed, upon my sword, indeed.
GHOST *(cries under the stage).* Swear.
HAMLET. Ah ha, boy, say'st thou so? Art thou there, truepenny?
Come on, you hear this fellow in the cellarage.
Consent to swear.
HORATIO. Propose the oath, my lord.
HAMLET. Never to speak of this that you have seen.
Swear by my sword.
GHOST. Swear. *(They swear.)*
HAMLET. Hic et ubique? Then we'll shift our ground.
Come hither, gentlemen,
And lay your hands again upon my sword.
Swear by my sword
Never to speak of this that you have heard.
GHOST. Swear by his sword. *(They swear.)*
HAMLET. Well said, old mole. Canst work i'th' earth so fast?
A worthy pioner! Once more remove, good friends.
HORATIO. O day and night, but this is wondrous strange.
HAMLET. And therefore as a stranger give it welcome.
There are more things in heaven and earth, Horatio,

Than are dreamt of in your philosophy.
But come,
Here, as before, never, so help you mercy,
How strange or odd some'er I bear myself –
As I perchance hereafter shall think meet
To put an antic disposition on –
That you, at such time seeing me, never shall,
With arms encumber'd thus, or this head-shake,
Or by pronouncing of some doubtful phrase,
As "Well, we know", or "We could and if we would",
Or "If we list to speak", or "There be and if they might",
Or such ambiguous giving out, to note
That you know aught of me – this do swear,
So grace and mercy at your most need help you.

GHOST. Swear. *(They swear.)*

HAMLET. Rest, rest, perturbed spirit. So, gentlemen,
With all my love I do commend me to you;
And what so poor a man as Hamlet is
May do t'express his love and friending to you,
God willing, shall not lack. Let us go in together.
And still your fingers on your lips, I pray.
The time is out of joint. O cursed spite,
That ever I was born to set it right.
Nay, come, let's go together. *(Exeunt.)*

ACT II

SCENE I

Enter old Polonius, with his man Reynaldo.

POLONIUS. Give him this money and these notes, Reynaldo.
REYNALDO. I will, my lord.
POLONIUS. You shall do marvellous wisely, good Reynaldo,
Before you visit him, to make inquire
Of his behaviour.
REYNALDO. My lord, I did intend it.
POLONIUS. Marry, well said, very well said. Look you, sir,
Inquire me first what Danskers are in Paris,
And how, and who, what means, and where they keep,
What company, at what expense; and finding
By this encompassment and drift of question
That they do know my son, come you more nearer
Than your particular demands will touch it.
Take you as 'twere some distant knowledge of him,
As thus, "I know his father, and his friends,
And in part him" – do you mark this, Reynaldo?
REYNALDO. Ay, very well, my lord.
POLONIUS. "And in part him. But", you may say, "not well;
But if't be he I mean, he's very wild,
Addicted so and so" – and there put on him
What forgeries you please – marry, none so rank
As may dishonour him – take heed of that –
But, sir, such wanton, wild, and usual slips
As are companions noted and most known
To youth and liberty.
REYNALDO.
As gaming, my lord?
POLONIUS. Ay, or drinking, fencing, swearing,
Quarrelling, drabbing – you may go so far.
REYNALDO. My lord, that would dishonour him.
POLONIUS. 'Faith no, as you may season it in the charge.
You must not put another scandal on him,
That he is open to incontinency –
That's not my meaning; but breathe his faults so quaintly
That they may seem the taints of liberty,
The flash and outbreak of a fiery mind,
A savageness in unreclaimed blood,

Of general assault.
REYNALDO.
But my good lord –
POLONIUS. Wherefore should you do this?
REYNALDO. Ay, my lord, I would know that.
POLONIUS. Marry, sir, here's my drift,
And I believe it is a fetch of warrant.
You laying these slight sullies on my son,
As 'twere a thing a little soil'd i'th' working,
Mark you,
Your party in converse, him you would sound,
Having ever seen in the prenominate crimes
The youth you breathe of guilty, be assur'd
He closes with you in this consequence:
"Good sir", or so, or "friend", or "gentleman",
According to the phrase or the addition
Of man and country.
REYNALDO. Very good, my lord.
POLONIUS. And then, sir, does a this – a does – what was I about to say? By the mass, I was about to say something. Where did I leave?
REYNALDO. At "closes in the consequence".
POLONIUS. At "closes in the consequence", ay, marry.
He closes thus: "I know the gentleman,
I saw him yesterday", or "th'other day",
Or then, or then, with such or such, "and as you say,
There was a gaming", "there o'ertook in's rouse",
"There falling out at tennis", or perchance
"I saw him enter such a house of sale" –
Videlicet a brothel, or so forth.
See you now,
Your bait of falsehood takes this carp of truth;
And thus do we of wisdom and of reach,
With windlasses and with assays of bias,
By indirections find directions out.
So by my former lecture and advice
Shall you my son. You have me, have you not?
REYNALDO. My lord, I have.
POLONIUS. God buy ye, fare ye well.
REYNALDO. Good my lord.
POLONIUS. Observe his inclination in yourself.
REYNALDO. I shall, my lord.
POLONIUS. And let him ply his music.

REYNALDO. Well, my lord. *(Exit.)*

(Enter Ophelia.)

POLONIUS. Farewell. How now, Ophelia, what's the matter?
OPHELIA. O my lord, my lord, I have been so affrighted.
POLONIUS. With what, i'th' name of God?
OPHELIA. My lord, as I was sewing in my closet,
Lord Hamlet, with his doublet all unbrac'd,
No hat upon his head, his stockings foul'd,
Ungarter'd and down-gyved to his ankle,
Pale as his shirt, his knees knocking each other,
And with a look so piteous in purport
As if he had been loosed out of hell
To speak of horrors, he comes before me.
POLONIUS. Mad for thy love?
OPHELIA. My lord, I do not know,
But truly I do fear it.
POLONIUS. What said he?
OPHELIA. He took me by the wrist and held me hard.
Then goes he to the length of all his arm,
And with his other hand thus o'er his brow
He falls to such perusal of my face
As a would draw it. Long stay'd he so.
At last, a little shaking of mine arm,
And thrice his head thus waving up and down,
He rais'd a sigh so piteous and profound
As it did seem to shatter all his bulk
And end his being. That done, he lets me go,
And with his head over his shoulder turn'd
He seem'd to find his way without his eyes,
For out o' doors he went without their helps,
And to the last bended their light on me.
POLONIUS. Come, go with me, I will go seek the King.
This is the very ecstasy of love,
Whose violent property fordoes itself
And leads the will to desperate undertakings
As oft as any passion under heaven
That does afflict our natures. I am sorry –
What, have you given him any hard words of late?
OPHELIA. No, my good lord, but as you did command,
I did repel his letters and denied
His access to me.
POLONIUS. That hath made him mad.
I am sorry that with better heed and judgment

I had not quoted him. I fear'd he did but trifle
And meant to wrack thee. But beshrew my jealousy!
By heaven, it is as proper to our age
To cast beyond ourselves in our opinions
As it is common for the younger sort
To lack discretion. Come, go we to the King.
This must be known, which, being kept close, might move
More grief to hide than hate to utter love.
Come.

(Exeunt.)

SCENE II

Flourish. Enter King and Queen, Rosencrantz and Guildenstern, with Attendants.

KING. Welcome, dear Rosencrantz and Guildenstern.
Moreover that we much did long to see you,
The need we have to use you did provoke
Our hasty sending. Something have you heard
Of Hamlet's transformation – so I call it,
Sith nor th'exterior nor the inward man
Resembles that it was. What it should be,
More than his father's death, that thus hath put him
So much from th'understanding of himself
I cannot dream of. I entreat you both
That, being of so young days brought up with him,
And sith so neighbour'd to his youth and haviour,
That you vouchsafe your rest here in our court
Some little time, so by your companies
To draw him on to pleasures and to gather,
So much as from occasion you may glean,
Whether aught to us unknown afflicts him thus
That, open'd, lies within our remedy.

QUEEN. Good gentlemen, he hath much talk'd of you,
And sure I am, two men there is not living
To whom he more adheres. If it will please you
To show us so much gentry and good will
As to expend your time with us awhile
For the supply and profit of our hope,
Your visitation shall receive such thanks
As fits a king's remembrance.

ROSENCRANTZ. Both your Majesties
Might, by the sovereign power you have of us,
Put your dread pleasures more into command
Than to entreaty.
GUILDENSTERN. But we both obey,
And here give up ourselves in the full bent
To lay our service freely at your feet
To be commanded.
KING. Thanks, Rosencrantz and gentle Guildenstern.
QUEEN. Thanks, Guildenstern and gentle Rosencrantz.
And I beseech you instantly to visit
My too much changed son. Go, some of you,
And bring these gentlemen where Hamlet is.
GUILDENSTERN. Heavens make our presence and our practices
Pleasant and helpful to him.
QUEEN. Ay, amen.
(Exeunt Rosencrantz and Guildenstern, and an Attendant.)
(Enter Polonius.)
POLONIUS. Th'ambassadors from Norway, my good lord,
Are joyfully return'd.
KING. Thou still hast been the father of good news.
POLONIUS. Have I, my lord? I assure my good liege
I hold my duty as I hold my soul,
Both to my God and to my gracious King;
And I do think – or else this brain of mine
Hunts not the trail of policy so sure
As it hath us'd to do – that I have found
The very cause of Hamlet's lunacy.
KING. O speak of that: that do I long to hear.
POLONIUS. Give first admittance to th'ambassadors.
My news shall be the fruit to that great feast.
KING. Thyself do grace to them and bring them in. *(Exit Polonius.)*
He tells me, my dear Gertrude, he hath found
The head and source of all your son's distemper.
QUEEN. I doubt it is no other but the main,
His father's death and our o'er-hasty marriage.
KING. Well, we shall sift him.
(Enter Polonius, Voltemand, and Cornelius.)
Welcome, my good friends.
Say, Voltemand, what from our brother Norway?
VOLTEMAND. Most fair return of greetings and desires.
Upon our first, he sent out to suppress
His nephew's levies, which to him appear'd

To be a preparation 'gainst the Polack;
But better look'd into, he truly found
It was against your Highness; whereat griev'd
That so his sickness, age, and impotence
Was falsely borne in hand, sends out arrests
On Fortinbras; which he, in brief, obeys,
Receives rebuke from Norway, and, in fine,
Makes vow before his uncle never more
To give th'assay of arms against your Majesty:
Whereon old Norway, overcome with joy,
Gives him three thousand crowns in annual fee
And his commission to employ those soldiers
So levied, as before, against the Polack,
With an entreaty, herein further shown, *(Gives a paper.)*
That it might please you to give quiet pass
Through your dominions for this enterprise
On such regards of safety and allowance
As therein are set down.

KING. It likes us well;
And at our more consider'd time we'll read,
Answer, and think upon this business.
Meantime, we thank you for your well-took labour.
Go to your rest, at night we'll feast together.
Most welcome home. *(Exeunt Voltemand and Cornelius.)*

POLONIUS. This business is well ended.
My liege and madam, to expostulate
What majesty should be, what duty is,
Why day is day, night night, and time is time,
Were nothing but to waste night, day, and time.
Therefore, since brevity is the soul of wit,
And tediousness the limbs and outward flourishes,
I will be brief. Your noble son is mad.
Mad call I it, for to define true madness,
What is't but to be nothing else but mad?
But let that go.

QUEEN. More matter with less art.

POLONIUS. Madam, I swear I use no art at all.
That he is mad 'tis true; 'tis true 'tis pity;
And pity 'tis 'tis true. A foolish figure –
But farewell it, for I will use no art.
Mad let us grant him then. And now remains
That we find out the cause of this effect,
Or rather say the cause of this defect,

For this effect defective comes by cause.
Thus it remains; and the remainder thus:
Perpend,
I have a daughter – have while she is mine –
Who in her duty and obedience, mark,
Hath given me this. Now gather and surmise.
(Reads) "To the celestial and my soul's idol, the most beautified Ophelia" – That's an ill phrase, a vile phrase, "beautified" is a vile phrase. But you shall hear – "these; in her excellent white bosom, these", &c.

QUEEN. Came this from Hamlet to her?

POLONIUS. Good madam, stay awhile, I will be faithful.
"Doubt thou the stars are fire,
Doubt that the sun doth move,
Doubt truth to be a liar,
But never doubt I love.
O dear Ophelia, I am ill at these numbers. I have not art to reckon my groans. But that I love thee best, O most best, believe it. Adieu.
Thine evermore, most dear lady, whilst this machine is to him,
Hamlet."
This in obedience hath my daughter shown me,
And, more above, hath his solicitings,
As they fell out by time, by means, and place,
All given to mine ear.

KING. But how hath she receiv'd his love?

POLONIUS. What do you think of me?

KING. As of a man faithful and honourable.

POLONIUS. I would fain prove so. But what might you think,
When I had seen this hot love on the wing –
As I perceiv'd it, I must tell you that,
Before my daughter told me – what might you
Or my dear Majesty your queen here think,
If I had play'd the desk or table-book,
Or given my heart a winking mute and dumb,
Or look'd upon this love with idle sight –
What might you think? No, I went round to work,
And my young mistress thus I did bespeak:
"Lord Hamlet is a prince out of thy star.
This must not be." And then I prescripts gave her,
That she should lock herself from his resort,
Admit no messengers, receive no tokens;
Which done, she took the fruits of my advice,

And he, repelled – a short tale to make –
Fell into a sadness, then into a fast,
Thence to a watch, thence into a weakness,
Thence to a lightness, and, by this declension,
Into the madness wherein now he raves
And all we mourn for.
KING. Do you think 'tis this?
QUEEN. It may be; very like.
POLONIUS.
Hath there been such a time – I would fain know that –
That I have positively said "'Tis so",
When it prov'd otherwise?
KING. Not that I know.
POLONIUS. Take this from this if this be otherwise.
(Points to his head and shoulder.)
If circumstances lead me, I will find
Where truth is hid, though it were hid indeed
Within the centre.
KING. How may we try it further?
POLONIUS. You know sometimes he walks four hours together
Here in the lobby.
QUEEN. So he does indeed.
POLONIUS. At such a time I'll loose my daughter to him.
Be you and I behind an arras then,
Mark the encounter. If he love her not,
And be not from his reason fall'n thereon,
Let me be no assistant for a state,
But keep a farm and carters.
KING. We will try it.
(Enter Hamlet, reading on a book.)
QUEEN. But look where sadly the poor wretch comes reading.
POLONIUS. Away, I do beseech you both, away.
I'll board him presently. O give me leave.
(Exeunt King and Queen, and Attendants.)
How does my good Lord Hamlet?
HAMLET. Well, God-a-mercy.
POLONIUS. Do you know me, my lord?
HAMLET. Excellent well. You are a fishmonger.
POLONIUS. Not I, my lord.
HAMLET. Then I would you were so honest a man.
POLONIUS. Honest, my lord?
HAMLET. Ay sir. To be honest, as this world goes, is to be one man picked out of ten thousand.

POLONIUS. That's very true, my lord.

HAMLET. For if the sun breed maggots in a dead dog, being a good kissing carrion – Have you a daughter?

POLONIUS. I have, my lord.

HAMLET. Let her not walk i'th' sun. Conception is a blessing, but as your daughter may conceive – friend, look to't.

POLONIUS *(aside).* How say you by that? Still harping on my daughter. Yet he knew me not at first; a said I was a fishmonger. A is far gone. And truly in my youth I suffered much extremity for love, very near this. I'll speak to him again. – What do you read, my lord?

HAMLET. Words, words, words.

POLONIUS. What is the matter, my lord?

HAMLET. Between who?

POLONIUS. I mean the matter that you read, my lord.

HAMLET. Slanders, sir. For the satirical rogue says here that old men have gray beards, that their faces are wrinkled, their eyes purging thick amber and plum-tree gum, and that they have a plentiful lack of wit, together with most weak hams – all which, sir, though I most powerfully and potently believe, yet I hold it not honesty to have it thus set down. For yourself, sir, shall grow old as I am – if like a crab you could go backward.

POLONIUS *(aside).* Though this be madness, yet there is method in't. – Will you walk out of the air, my lord?

HAMLET. Into my grave?

POLONIUS. Indeed, that's out of the air. – *(Aside)* How pregnant sometimes his replies are – a happiness that often madness hits on, which reason and sanity could not so prosperously be delivered of. I will leave him and suddenly contrive the means of meeting between him and my daughter. – My lord, I will take my leave of you.

HAMLET. You cannot, sir, take from me anything that I will not more willingly part withal – except my life, except my life, except my life.

POLONIUS. Fare you well, my lord.

HAMLET. These tedious old fools.

(Enter Rosencrantz and Guildenstern.)

POLONIUS. You go to seek the Lord Hamlet. There he is.

ROSENCRANTZ. God save you, sir. *(Exit Polonius.)*

GUILDENSTERN. My honoured lord.

ROSENCRANTZ. My most dear lord.

HAMLET. My excellent good friends. How dost thou, Guildenstern? Ah, Rosencrantz. Good lads, how do you both?

ROSENCRANTZ. As the indifferent children of the earth.

GUILDENSTERN. Happy in that we are not over-happy: on Fortune's cap we are not the very button.

HAMLET. Nor the soles of her shoe?

ROSENCRANTZ. Neither, my lord.

HAMLET. Then you live about her waist, or in the middle of her favours?

GUILDENSTERN. Faith, her privates we.

HAMLET. In the secret parts of Fortune? O most true, she is a strumpet. What news?

ROSENCRANTZ.
None, my lord, but the world's grown honest.

HAMLET. Then is doomsday near. But your news is not true. Let me question more in particular. What have you, my good friends, deserved at the hands of Fortune that she sends you to prison hither?

GUILDENSTERN. Prison, my lord?

HAMLET. Denmark's a prison.

ROSENCRANTZ. Then is the world one.

HAMLET. A goodly one, in which there are many confines, wards, and dungeons, Denmark being one o'th' worst.

ROSENCRANTZ. We think not so, my lord.

HAMLET. Why, then 'tis none to you; for there is nothing either good or bad but thinking makes it so. To me it is a prison.

ROSENCRANTZ. Why, then your ambition makes it one: 'tis too narrow for your mind.

HAMLET. O God, I could be bounded in a nutshell and count myself a king of infinite space – were it not that I have bad dreams.

GUILDENSTERN. Which dreams indeed are ambition; for the very substance of the ambitious is merely the shadow of a dream.

HAMLET. A dream itself is but a shadow.

ROSENCRANTZ. Truly, and I hold ambition of so airy and light a quality that it is but a shadow's shadow.

HAMLET. Then are our beggars bodies, and our monarchs and outstretched heroes the beggars' shadows. Shall we to th' court? For by my fay, I cannot reason.

ROSENCRANTZ AND GUILDENSTERN.
We'll wait upon you.

HAMLET. No such matter. I will not sort you with the rest of my servants; for, to speak to you like an honest man, I am most dreadfully attended. But in the beaten way of friendship, what make you at Elsinore?

ROSENCRANTZ. To visit you, my lord, no other occasion.

HAMLET. Beggar that I am, I am even poor in thanks, but I thank you. And sure, dear friends, my thanks are too dear a halfpenny. Were you not sent for? Is it your own inclining? Is it a free visitation? Come, come, deal justly with me. Come, come. Nay, speak.

GUILDENSTERN. What should we say, my lord?

HAMLET. Anything but to th' purpose. You were sent for, and there is a kind of confession in your looks, which your modesties have not craft enough to colour. I know the good King and Queen have sent for you.

ROSENCRANTZ. To what end, my lord?

HAMLET. That, you must teach me. But let me conjure you, by the rights of our fellowship, by the consonancy of our youth, by the obligation of our ever-preserved love, and by what more dear a better proposer can charge you withal, be even and direct with me whether you were sent for or no.

ROSENCRANTZ *(aside to Guildenstern).* What say you?

HAMLET. Nay, then I have an eye of you. If you love me, hold not off.

GUILDENSTERN. My lord, we were sent for.

HAMLET. I will tell you why; so shall my anticipation prevent your discovery, and your secrecy to the King and Queen moult no feather. I have of late, but wherefore I know not, lost all my mirth, forgone all custom of exercises; and indeed it goes so heavily with my disposition that this goodly frame the earth seems to me a sterile promontory, this most excellent canopy the air, look you, this brave o'erhanging firmament, this majestical roof fretted with golden fire, why, it appeareth nothing to me but a foul and pestilent congregation of vapours. What piece of work is a man, how noble in reason, how infinite in faculties, in form and moving how express and admirable, in action how like an angel, in apprehension how like a god: the beauty of the world, the paragon of animals – and yet, to me, what is this quintessence of dust? Man delights not me – nor woman neither, though by your smiling you seem to say so.

ROSENCRANTZ. My lord, there was no such stuff in my thoughts.

HAMLET. Why did ye laugh then, when I said man delights not me?

ROSENCRANTZ. To think, my lord, if you delight not in man, what Lenten entertainment the players shall receive from you. We coted them on the way, and hither are they coming to offer you service.

HAMLET. He that plays the king shall be welcome – his Majesty shall have tribute on me, the adventurous knight shall use his foil and target, the lover shall not sigh gratis, the humorous man shall end his part in peace, the clown shall make those laugh whose lungs are tickle a th' sear, and the lady shall say her mind freely – or the blank verse shall halt for't. What players are they?

ROSENCRANTZ. Even those you were wont to take such delight in, the tragedians of the city.

HAMLET. How chances it they travel? Their residence, both in reputation and profit, was better both ways.

ROSENCRANTZ. I think their inhibition comes by the means of the late innovation.

HAMLET. Do they hold the same estimation they did when I was in the city? Are they so followed?

ROSENCRANTZ. No, indeed are they not.

HAMLET. How comes it? Do they grow rusty?

ROSENCRANTZ. Nay, their endeavour keeps in the wonted pace; but there is, sir, an eyrie of children, little eyases, that cry out on the top of question, and are most tyrannically clapped for't. These are now the fashion, and so berattle the common stages – so they call them – that many wearing rapiers are afraid of goose-quills and dare scarce come thither.

HAMLET. What, are they children? Who maintains 'em? How are they escotted? Will they pursue the quality no longer than they can sing? Will they not say afterwards, if they should grow themselves to common players – as it is most like, if their means are no better – their writers do them wrong to make them exclaim against their own succession?

ROSENCRANTZ. Faith, there has been much to do on both sides; and the nation holds it no sin to tar them to controversy. There was for a while no money bid for argument unless the poet and the player went to cuffs in the question.

HAMLET. Is't possible?

GUILDENSTERN. O, there has been much throwing about of brains.

HAMLET. Do the boys carry it away?

ROSENCRANTZ. Ay, that they do, my lord, Hercules and his load too.

HAMLET. It is not very strange; for my uncle is King of Denmark, and those that would make mouths at him while my father lived give twenty, forty, fifty, a hundred ducats apiece for his picture in little. 'Sblood, there is something in this more than natural, if philosophy could find it out. *(A flourish of trumpets.)*

GUILDENSTERN. There are the players.

HAMLET. Gentlemen, you are welcome to Elsinore. Your hands, come then. Th'appurtenance of welcome is fashion and ceremony. Let me comply with you in this garb – lest my extent to the players, which I tell you must show fairly outwards, should more appear like entertainment than yours. You are welcome. But my uncle-father and aunt-mother are deceived.

GUILDENSTERN. In what, my dear lord?

HAMLET. I am but mad north-north-west. When the wind is southerly, I know a hawk from a handsaw.

(Enter Polonius.)

POLONIUS. Well be with you, gentlemen.

HAMLET. Hark you, Guildenstern, and you too – at each ear a hearer. That great baby you see there is not yet out of his swaddling-clouts.

ROSENCRANTZ. Happily he is the second time come to them, for they say an old man is twice a child.

HAMLET. I will prophesy he comes to tell me of the players. Mark it. – You say right, sir, a Monday morning, 'twas then indeed.

POLONIUS. My lord, I have news to tell you.

HAMLET. My lord, I have news to tell you. When Roscius was an actor in Rome –

POLONIUS. The actors are come hither, my lord.

HAMLET. Buzz, buzz.

POLONIUS. Upon my honour –

HAMLET. "Then came each actor on his ass" –

POLONIUS. The best actors in the world, either for tragedy, comedy, history, pastoral, pastoral-comical, historical-pastoral, tragical-historical, tragical-comical-historical-pastoral, scene individable, or poem unlimited. Seneca cannot be too heavy, nor Plautus too light. For the law of writ, and the liberty, these are the only men.

HAMLET. "O Jephthah, judge of Israel", what a treasure hadst thou!

POLONIUS. What a treasure had he, my lord?

HAMLET. Why,

"One fair daughter and no more,
The which he loved passing well."

POLONIUS *(aside)*. Still on my daughter.

HAMLET. Am I not i 'th' right, old Jephthah?

POLONIUS. If you call me Jephthah, my lord, I have a daughter that I love passing well.

HAMLET. Nay, that follows not.
POLONIUS. What follows then, my lord?
HAMLET. Why,
"As by lot God wot",
and then, you know,
"It came to pass, as most like it was".
The first row of the pious chanson will show you more, for look where my abridgement comes.

(Enter the Players.)

You are welcome, masters. Welcome, all. – I am glad to see thee well. – Welcome, good friends. – O, old friend, why, thy face is valanced since I saw thee last. Com'st thou to beard me in Denmark? – What, my young lady and mistress! By'r lady, your ladyship is nearer to heaven than when I saw you last by the altitude of a chopine. Pray God your voice, like a piece of uncurrent gold, be not cracked within the ring. – Masters, you are all welcome. We'll e'en to't like French falconers, fly at anything we see. We'll have a speech straight. Come, give us a taste of your quality. Come, a passionate speech.
FIRST PLAYER. What speech, my good lord?
HAMLET. I heard thee speak me a speech once, but it was never acted, or if it was, not above once – for the play, I remember, pleased not the million, 'twas caviare to the general. But it was, as I received it – and others, whose judgments in such matters cried in the top of mine – an excellent play, well digested in the scenes, set down with as much modesty as cunning. I remember one said there were no sallets in the lines to make the matter savoury, nor no matter in the phrase that might indict the author of affection, but called it an honest method, as wholesome as sweet, and by very much more handsome than fine. One speech in't I chiefly loved – 'twas Aeneas' tale to Dido – and thereabout of it especially when he speaks of Priam's slaughter. If it live in your memory, begin at this line – let me see, let me see –
"The rugged Pyrrhus, like th'Hyrcanian beast" –
'Tis not so. It begins with Pyrrhus –
"The rugged Pyrrhus, he whose sable arms,
Black as his purpose, did the night resemble
When he lay couched in the ominous horse,
Hath now this dread and black complexion smear'd
With heraldry more dismal. Head to foot
Now is he total gules, horridly trick'd
With blood of fathers, mothers, daughters, sons,

Bak'd and impasted with the parching streets,
That lend a tyrannous and a damned light
To their lord's murder. Roasted in wrath and fire,
And thus o'ersized with coagulate gore,
With eyes like carbuncles, the hellish Pyrrhus
Old grandsire Priam seeks."
So proceed you.

POLONIUS. 'Fore God, my lord, well spoken, with good accent and good discretion.

FIRST PLAYER. "Anon he finds him,
Striking too short at Greeks. His antique sword,
Rebellious to his arm, lies where it falls,
Repugnant to command. Unequal match'd,
Pyrrhus at Priam drives, in rage strikes wide;
But with the whiff and wind of his fell sword
Th'unnerved father falls. Then senseless Ilium,
Seeming to feel this blow, with flaming top
Stoops to his base, and with a hideous crash
Takes prisoner Pyrrhus' ear. For lo, his sword,
Which was declining on the milky head
Of reverend Priam, seem'd i'th' air to stick;
So, as a painted tyrant, Pyrrhus stood,
And like a neutral to his will and matter,
Did nothing.
But as we often see against some storm
A silence in the heavens, the rack stand still,
The bold winds speechless, and the orb below
As hush as death, anon the dreadful thunder
Doth rend the region; so after Pyrrhus' pause
Aroused vengeance sets him new awork,
And never did the Cyclops' hammers fall
On Mars's armour, forg'd for proof eterne,
With less remorse than Pyrrhus' bleeding sword
Now falls on Priam.
Out, out, thou strumpet Fortune! All you gods
In general synod take away her power,
Break all the spokes and fellies from her wheel,
And bowl the round nave down the hill of heaven
As low as to the fiends."

POLONIUS. This is too long.

HAMLET. It shall to the barber's with your beard. – Prithee say on. He's for a jig or a tale of bawdry, or he sleeps. Say on, come to Hecuba.

FIRST PLAYER.
"But who – ah, woe ! – had seen the mobbled queen" –

HAMLET. "The mobbled queen".

POLONIUS. That's good.

FIRST PLAYER.
"Run barefoot up and down, threat'ning the flames
With bisson rheum, a clout upon that head
Where late the diadem stood, and, for a robe,
About her lank and all o'erteemed loins
A blanket, in th'alarm of fear caught up –
Who this had seen, with tongue in venom steep'd,
'Gainst Fortune's state would treason have pronounc'd.
But if the gods themselves did see her then,
When she saw Pyrrhus make malicious sport
In mincing with his sword her husband's limbs,
The instant burst of clamour that she made,
Unless things mortal move them not at all,
Would have made milch the burning eyes of heaven
And passion in the gods."

POLONIUS. Look whe'er he has not turned his colour and has tears in's eyes. Prithee no more.

HAMLET. 'Tis well. I'll have thee speak out the rest of this soon. – Good my lord, will you see the players well bestowed? Do you hear, let them be well used, for they are the abstract and brief chronicles of the time. After your death you were better have a bad epitaph than their ill report while you live.

POLONIUS. My lord, I will use them according to their desert.

HAMLET. God's bodkin, man, much better. Use every man after his desert, and who shall scape whipping? Use them after your own honour and dignity: the less they deserve, the more merit is in your bounty. Take them in.

POLONIUS. Come, sirs.

HAMLET. Follow him, friends. We'll hear a play tomorrow. *(To First Player)* Dost thou hear me, old friend? Can you play The Murder of Gonzago?

FIRST PLAYER. Ay, my lord.

HAMLET. We'll ha't tomorrow night. You could for a need study a speech of some dozen or sixteen lines, which I would set down and insert in't, could you not?

FIRST PLAYER. Ay, my lord.

HAMLET. Very well. *(To all the Players)* Follow that lord, and look you mock him not. *(Exeunt Polonius and Players.)* *(To Rosencrantz and Guildenstern)* My good friends,

I'll leave you till night. You are welcome to Elsinore.
ROSENCRANTZ. Good my lord.
(Exeunt Rosencrantz and Guildenstern.)
HAMLET. Ay, so, God buy to you. Now I am alone.
O what a rogue and peasant slave am I!
Is it not monstrous that this player here,
But in a fiction, in a dream of passion,
Could force his soul so to his own conceit
That from her working all his visage wann'd,
Tears in his eyes, distraction in his aspect,
A broken voice, and his whole function suiting
With forms to his conceit? And all for nothing!
For Hecuba!
What's Hecuba to him, or he to her,
That he should weep for her? What would he do
Had he the motive and the cue for passion
That I have? He would drown the stage with tears,
And cleave the general ear with horrid speech,
Make mad the guilty and appal the free,
Confound the ignorant, and amaze indeed
The very faculties of eyes and ears.
Yet I,
A dull and muddy-mettled rascal, peak
Like John-a-dreams, unpregnant of my cause,
And can say nothing – no, not for a king,
Upon whose property and most dear life
A damn'd defeat was made. Am I a coward?
Who calls me villain, breaks my pate across,
Plucks off my beard and blows it in my face,
Tweaks me by the nose, gives me the lie i'th' throat
As deep as to the lungs – who does me this?
Ha!
'Swounds, I should take it: for it cannot be
But I am pigeon-liver'd and lack gall
To make oppression bitter, or ere this
I should ha' fatted all the region kites
With this slave's offal. Bloody, bawdy villain!
Remorseless, treacherous, lecherous, kindless villain!
Why, what an ass am I! This is most brave,
That I, the son of a dear father murder'd,
Prompted to my revenge by heaven and hell,
Must like a whore unpack my heart with words
And fall a-cursing like a very drab,

A scullion! Fie upon't! Foh!
About, my brains. Hum – I have heard
That guilty creatures sitting at a play
Have, by the very cunning of the scene,
Been struck so to the soul that presently
They have proclaim'd their malefactions.
For murder, though it have no tongue, will speak
With most miraculous organ. I'll have these players
Play something like the murder of my father
Before mine uncle. I'll observe his looks;
I'll tent him to the quick. If a do blench,
I know my course. The spirit that I have seen
May be a devil, and the devil hath power
T'assume a pleasing shape, yea, and perhaps,
Out of my weakness and my melancholy,
As he is very potent with such spirits,
Abuses me to damn me. I'll have grounds
More relative than this. The play's the thing
Wherein I'll catch the conscience of the King.

(Exit.)

ACT III

SCENE I

Enter King, Queen, Polonius, Ophelia, Rosencrantz, Guildenstern.

KING. And can you by no drift of conference
Get from him why he puts on this confusion,
Grating so harshly all his days of quiet
With turbulent and dangerous lunacy?
ROSENCRANTZ. He does confess he feels himself distracted,
But from what cause a will by no means speak.
GUILDENSTERN. Nor do we find him forward to be sounded,
But with a crafty madness keeps aloof
When we would bring him on to some confession
Of his true state.
QUEEN. Did he receive you well?
ROSENCRANTZ. Most like a gentleman.
GUILDENSTERN. But with much forcing of his disposition.
ROSENCRANTZ. Niggard of question, but of our demands
Most free in his reply.
QUEEN. Did you assay him
To any pastime?
ROSENCRANTZ. Madam, it so fell out that certain players
We o'erraught on the way. Of these we told him,
And there did seem in him a kind of joy
To hear of it. They are here about the court,
And, as I think, they have already order
This night to play before him.
POLONIUS. 'Tis most true,
And he beseech'd me to entreat your Majesties
To hear and see the matter.
KING. With all my heart; and it doth much content me
To hear him so inclin'd.
Good gentlemen, give him a further edge,
And drive his purpose into these delights.
ROSENCRANTZ.
We shall, my lord. *(Exeunt Rosencrantz and Guildenstern.)*
KING. Sweet Gertrude, leave us too,
For we have closely sent for Hamlet hither
That he, as 'twere by accident, may here
Affront Ophelia.

Her father and myself, lawful espials,
We'll so bestow ourselves that, seeing unseen,
We may of their encounter frankly judge,
And gather by him, as he is behav'd,
If't be th'affliction of his love or no
That thus he suffers for.

QUEEN. I shall obey you.
And for your part, Ophelia, I do wish
That your good beauties be the happy cause
Of Hamlet's wildness; so shall I hope your virtues
Will bring him to his wonted way again,
To both your honours.

OPHELIA. Madam, I wish it may. *(Exit Queen.)*

POLONIUS. Ophelia, walk you here. – Gracious, so please you,
We will bestow ourselves. – Read on this book,
That show of such an exercise may colour
Your loneliness. – We are oft to blame in this,
'Tis too much prov'd, that with devotion's visage
And pious action we do sugar o'er
The devil himself.

KING *(aside).* O 'tis too true.
How smart a lash that speech doth give my conscience.
The harlot's cheek, beautied with plast'ring art,
Is not more ugly to the thing that helps it
Than is my deed to my most painted word.
O heavy burden!

POLONIUS. I hear him coming. Let's withdraw, my lord.
(Exeunt King and Polonius.)

(Enter Hamlet.)

HAMLET. To be, or not to be, that is the question:
Whether 'tis nobler in the mind to suffer
The slings and arrows of outrageous fortune,
Or to take arms against a sea of troubles
And by opposing end them. To die – to sleep,
No more; and by a sleep to say we end
The heart-ache and the thousand natural shocks
That flesh is heir to: 'tis a consummation
Devoutly to be wish'd. To die, to sleep;
To sleep, perchance to dream – ay, there's the rub:
For in that sleep of death what dreams may come,
When we have shuffled off this mortal coil,
Must give us pause – there's the respect
That makes calamity of so long life.

For who would bear the whips and scorns of time,
Th'oppressor's wrong, the proud man's contumely,
The pangs of dispriz'd love, the law's delay,
The insolence of office, and the spurns
That patient merit of th'unworthy takes,
When he himself might his quietus make
With a bare bodkin? Who would fardels bear,
To grunt and sweat under a weary life,
But that the dread of something after death,
The undiscover'd country, from whose bourn
No traveller returns, puzzles the will,
And makes us rather bear those ills we have
Than fly to others that we know not of?
Thus conscience does make cowards of us all,
And thus the native hue of resolution
Is sicklied o'er with the pale cast of thought,
And enterprises of great pitch and moment
With this regard their currents turn awry
And lose the name of action. Soft you now,
The fair Ophelia! Nymph, in thy orisons
Be all my sins remember'd.
OPHELIA. Good my lord,
How does your honour for this many a day?
HAMLET. I humbly thank you, well.
OPHELIA. My lord, I have remembrances of yours
That I have longed long to redeliver.
I pray you now receive them.
HAMLET. No, not I.
I never gave you aught.
OPHELIA. My honour'd lord, you know right well you did,
And with them words of so sweet breath compos'd
As made the things more rich. Their perfume lost,
Take these again; for to the noble mind
Rich gifts wax poor when givers prove unkind.
There, my lord.
HAMLET. Ha, ha! Are you honest?
OPHELIA. My lord?
HAMLET. Are you fair?
OPHELIA. What means your lordship?
HAMLET. That if you be honest and fair, your honesty should admit no discourse to your beauty.
OPHELIA. Could beauty, my lord, have better commerce than with honesty?

HAMLET. Ay, truly, for the power of beauty will sooner transform honesty from what it is to a bawd than the force of honesty can translate beauty into his likeness. This was sometime a paradox, but now the time gives it proof. I did love you once.

OPHELIA. Indeed, my lord, you made me believe so.

HAMLET. You should not have believed me; for virtue cannot so inoculate our old stock but we shall relish of it. I loved you not.

OPHELIA. I was the more deceived.

HAMLET. Get thee to a nunnery. Why, wouldst thou be a breeder of sinners? I am myself indifferent honest, but yet I could accuse me of such things that it were better my mother had not borne me. I am very proud, revengeful, ambitious, with more offences at my beck than I have thoughts to put them in, imagination to give them shape, or time to act them in. What should such fellows as I do crawling between earth and heaven? We are arrant knaves all, believe none of us. Go thy ways to a nunnery. Where's your father?

OPHELIA. At home, my lord.

HAMLET. Let the doors be shut upon him, that he may play the fool nowhere but in's own house. Farewell.

OPHELIA. O help him, you sweet heavens.

HAMLET. If thou dost marry, I'll give thee this plague for thy dowry: be thou as chaste as ice, as pure as snow, thou shalt not escape calumny. Get thee to a nunnery, farewell. Or if thou wilt needs marry, marry a fool; for wise men know well enough what monsters you make of them. To a nunnery, go – and quickly too. Farewell.

OPHELIA. Heavenly powers, restore him.

HAMLET. I have heard of your paintings well enough. God hath given you one face and you make yourselves another. You jig and amble, and you lisp, you nickname God's creatures, and make your wantonness your ignorance. Go to, I'll no more on't, it hath made me mad. I say we will have no mo marriage. Those that are married already – all but one – shall live; the rest shall keep as they are. To a nunnery, go. *(Exit.)*

OPHELIA. O, what a noble mind is here o'erthrown!
The courtier's, soldier's, scholar's, eye, tongue, sword,
Th'expectancy and rose of the fair state,
The glass of fashion and the mould of form,
Th'observ'd of all observers, quite, quite down!
And I, of ladies most deject and wretched,
That suck'd the honey of his music vows,
Now see that noble and most sovereign reason
Like sweet bells jangled out of tune and harsh,

That unmatch'd form and feature of blown youth
Blasted with ecstasy. O woe is me
T'have seen what I have seen, see what I see.
(Enter King and Polonius.)

KING. Love? His affections do not that way tend,
Nor what he spake, though it lack'd form a little,
Was not like madness. There's something in his soul
O'er which his melancholy sits on brood,
And I do doubt the hatch and the disclose
Will be some danger; which for to prevent,
I have in quick determination
Thus set it down: he shall with speed to England
For the demand of our neglected tribute.
Haply the seas and countries different,
With variable objects, shall expel
This something settled matter in his heart,
Whereon his brains still beating puts him thus
From fashion of himself. What think you on't?

POLONIUS. It shall do well. But yet do I believe
The origin and commencement of his grief
Sprung from neglected love. How now, Ophelia?
You need not tell us what Lord Hamlet said,
We heard it all. My lord, do as you please,
But if you hold it fit, after the play
Let his queen-mother all alone entreat him
To show his grief, let her be round with him,
And I'll be plac'd, so please you, in the ear
Of all their conference. If she find him not,
To England send him; or confine him where
Your wisdom best shall think.

KING. It shall be so.
Madness in great ones must not unwatch'd go. *(Exeunt.)*

SCENE II

Enter Hamlet and three of the Players. .

HAMLET. Speak the speech, I pray you, as I pronounced it to you, trippingly on the tongue; but if you mouth it as many of your players do, I had as lief the town-crier spoke my lines. Nor do not saw the air too much with your hand, thus, but use all gently; for in the very torrent, tempest, and, as I may say, whirlwind of your passion, you must acquire and beget a temperance that may give it smoothness. O, it offends me to the soul to hear a robustious periwig-pated fellow tear a passion to tatters, to very rags, to split the ears of the groundlings, who for the most part are capable of nothing but inexplicable dumb-shows and noise. I would have such a fellow whipped for o'erdoing Termagant. It out-Herods Herod. Pray you avoid it.

FIRST PLAYER. I warrant your honour.

HAMLET. Be not too tame neither, but let your own discretion be your tutor. Suit the action to the word, the word to the action, with this special observance, that you o'erstep not the modesty of nature. For anything so o'erdone is from the purpose of playing, whose end, both at the first and now, was and is to hold as 'twere the mirror up to nature; to show virtue her feature, scorn her own image, and the very age and body of the time his form and pressure. Now this overdone or come tardy off, though it makes the unskilful laugh, cannot but make the judicious grieve, the censure of the which one must in your allowance o'erweigh a whole theatre of others. O, there be players that I have seen play – and heard others praise, and that highly – not to speak it profanely, that neither having th'accent of Christians, nor the gait of Christian, pagan, nor man, have so strutted and bellowed that I have thought some of Nature's journeymen had made men, and not made them well, they imitated humanity so abominably.

FIRST PLAYER. I hope we have reformed that indifferently with us.

HAMLET. O reform it altogether. And let those that play your clowns speak no more than is set down for them – for there be of them that will themselves laugh, to set on some quantity of barren spectators to laugh too, though in the meantime some necessary question of the play be then to be considered. That's villainous, and shows a most pitiful ambition in the fool that uses it. Go make you ready. *(Exeunt Players.)*

(Enter Polonius, Rosencrantz, and Guildenstern.)

How now, my lord? Will the King hear this piece of work?

POLONIUS. And the Queen too, and that presently.

HAMLET. Bid the players make haste. *(Exit Polonius.)*
Will you two help to hasten them?

ROSENCRANTZ. Ay, my lord.

(Exeunt Rosencrantz and Guildenstern.)

HAMLET. What ho, Horatio!

(Enter Horatio.)

HORATIO. Here, sweet lord, at your service.

HAMLET. Horatio, thou art e'en as just a man

As e'er my conversation cop'd withal.
HORATIO. O my dear lord.
HAMLET. Nay, do not think I flatter,
For what advancement may I hope from thee
That no revenue hast but thy good spirits
To feed and clothe thee? Why should the poor be flatter'd?
No, let the candied tongue lick absurd pomp,
And crook the pregnant hinges of the knee
Where thrift may follow fawning. Dost thou hear?
Since my dear soul was mistress of her choice,
And could of men distinguish her election,
Sh'ath seal'd thee for herself; for thou hast been
As one, in suff'ring all, that suffers nothing,
A man that Fortune's buffets and rewards
Hast ta'en with equal thanks; and blest are those
Whose blood and judgment are so well commeddled
That they are not a pipe for Fortune's finger
To sound what stop she please. Give me that man
That is not passion's slave, and I will wear him
In my heart's core, ay, in my heart of heart,
As I do thee. Something too much of this.
There is a play tonight before the King:
One scene of it comes near the circumstance
Which I have told thee of my father's death.
I prithee, when thou seest that act afoot,
Even with the very comment of thy soul
Observe my uncle. If his occulted guilt
Do not itself unkennel in one speech,
It is a damned ghost that we have seen,
And my imaginations are as foul
As Vulcan's stithy. Give him heedful note;
For I mine eyes will rivet to his face,
And after we will both our judgments join
In censure of his seeming.
HORATIO. Well, my lord.
If a steal aught the whilst this play is playing
And scape detecting, I will pay the theft.
(Enter Trumpets and Kettle-drums and sound a flourish.)
HAMLET. They are coming to the play. I must be idle.
Get you a place.
(Enter King, Queen, Polonius, Ophelia, Rosencrantz, Guildenstern, and other Lords attendant, with the King's Guard carrying torches.)

KING. How fares our cousin Hamlet?

HAMLET. Excellent, i'faith, of the chameleon's dish. I eat the air, promise-crammed. You cannot feed capons so.

KING. I have nothing with this answer, Hamlet. These words are not mine.

HAMLET. No, nor mine now. – *(To Polonius)* My lord, you played once i'th' university, you say?

POLONIUS. That did I, my lord, and was accounted a good actor.

HAMLET. What did you enact?

POLONIUS. I did enact Julius Caesar. I was killed i'th' Capitol. Brutus killed me.

HAMLET. It was a brute part of him to kill so capital a calf there. Be the players ready?

ROSENCRANTZ. Ay, my lord, they stay upon your patience.

QUEEN. Come hither, my dear Hamlet, sit by me.

HAMLET. No, good mother, here's metal more attractive.

(Turns to Ophelia.)

POLONIUS *(aside to the King).* O ho! do you mark that?

HAMLET *(lying down at Ophelia's feet).* Lady, shall I lie in your lap?

OPHELIA. No, my lord.

HAMLET. I mean, my head upon your lap.

OPHELIA. Ay, my lord.

HAMLET. Do you think I meant country matters?

OPHELIA. I think nothing, my lord.

HAMLET. That's a fair thought to lie between maids' legs.

OPHELIA. What is, my lord?

HAMLET. Nothing.

OPHELIA. You are merry, my lord.

HAMLET. Who, I?

OPHELIA. Ay, my lord.

HAMLET. O God, your only jig-maker. What should a man do but be merry? For look you how cheerfully my mother looks and my father died within's two hours.

OPHELIA. Nay, 'tis twice two months, my lord.

HAMLET. So long? Nay then, let the devil wear black, for I'll have a suit of sables. O heavens, die two months ago and not forgotten yet! Then there's hope a great man's memory may outlive his life half a year. But by'r lady a must build churches then, or else shall a suffer not thinking on, with the hobby-horse, whose epitaph is "For O, for O, the hobby-horse is forgot".

(The trumpets sound. A dumb-show follows.)

(Enter a King and a Queen, the Queen embracing him and he her. She kneels, and makes show of protestation unto him. He takes her up, and declines his head upon her neck. He lies him down upon a bank of flowers. She, seeing him asleep, leaves him. Anon comes in another Man, takes off his crown, kisses it, pours poison in the sleeper's ears, and leaves him. The Queen returns, finds the King dead, makes passionate action. The Poisoner with some Three or Four comes in again. They seem to condole with her. The dead body is carried away. The Poisoner woos the Queen with gifts. She seems harsh awhile, but in the end accepts his love.)

(Exeunt.)

OPHELIA. What means this, my lord?
HAMLET. Marry, this is miching malicho. It means mischief.
OPHELIA. Belike this show imports the argument of the play.

(Enter Prologue.)

HAMLET. We shall know by this fellow. The players cannot keep counsel: they'll tell all.
OPHELIA. Will a tell us what this show meant?
HAMLET. Ay, or any show that you will show him. Be not you ashamed to show, he'll not shame to tell you what it means.
OPHELIA. You are naught, you are naught. I'll mark the play.
PROLOGUE. For us and for our tragedy,
Here stooping to your clemency,
We beg your hearing patiently. *(Exit.)*
HAMLET. Is this a prologue, or the posy of a ring?
OPHELIA. 'Tis brief, my lord.
HAMLET. As woman's love.

(Enter the Player King and Queen.)

PLAYER KING. Full thirty times hath Phoebus' cart gone round
Neptune's salt wash and Tellus' orbed ground,
And thirty dozen moons with borrow'd sheen
About the world have times twelve thirties been
Since love our hearts and Hymen did our hands
Unite commutual in most sacred bands.
PLAYER QUEEN. So many journeys may the sun and moon
Make us again count o'er ere love be done.
But woe is me, you are so sick of late,
So far from cheer and from your former state,
That I distrust you. Yet though I distrust,
Discomfort you, my lord, it nothing must;
For women's fear and love hold quantity,
In neither aught, or in extremity.

Now what my love is, proof hath made you know,
And as my love is siz'd, my fear is so.
Where love is great, the littlest doubts are fear;
Where little fears grow great, great love grows there.
PLAYER KING. Faith, I must leave thee, love, and shortly too:
My operant powers their functions leave to do;
And thou shalt live in this fair world behind,
Honour'd, belov'd; and haply one as kind
For husband shall thou –
PLAYER QUEEN. O confound the rest.
Such love must needs be treason in my breast.
In second husband let me be accurst;
None wed the second but who kill'd the first.
HAMLET *(aside).* That's wormwood.
PLAYER QUEEN. The instances that second marriage move
Are base respects of thrift, but none of love.
A second time I kill my husband dead,
When second husband kisses me in bed.
PLAYER KING. I do believe you think what now you speak;
But what we do determine, oft we break.
Purpose is but the slave to memory,
Of violent birth but poor validity,
Which now, the fruit unripe, sticks on the tree,
But fall unshaken when they mellow be.
Most necessary 'tis that we forget
To pay ourselves what to ourselves is debt.
What to ourselves in passion we propose,
The passion ending, doth the purpose lose.
The violence of either grief or joy
Their own enactures with themselves destroy.
Where joy most revels grief doth most lament;
Grief joys, joy grieves, on slender accident.
This world is not for aye, nor 'tis not strange
That even our loves should with our fortunes change,
For 'tis a question left us yet to prove,
Whether love lead fortune or else fortune love.
The great man down, you mark his favourite flies;
The poor advanc'd makes friends of enemies;
And hitherto doth love on fortune tend:
For who not needs shall never lack a friend,
And who in want a hollow friend doth try
Directly seasons him his enemy.
But orderly to end where I begun,

Our wills and fates do so contrary run
That our devices still are overthrown:
Our thoughts are ours, their ends none of our own.
So think thou wilt no second husband wed,
But die thy thoughts when thy first lord is dead.

PLAYER QUEEN. Nor earth to me give food, nor heaven light,
Sport and repose lock from me day and night,
To desperation turn my trust and hope,
An anchor's cheer in prison be my scope,
Each opposite, that blanks the face of joy,
Meet what I would have well and it destroy,
Both here and hence pursue me lasting strife,
If, once a widow, ever I be a wife.

HAMLET. If she should break it now.

PLAYER KING. 'Tis deeply sworn. Sweet, leave me here awhile.
My spirits grow dull, and fain I would beguile
The tedious day with sleep.

PLAYER QUEEN. Sleep rock thy brain,
And never come mischance between us twain. *(Exit. He sleeps.)*

HAMLET. Madam, how like you this play?

QUEEN. The lady doth protest too much, methinks.

HAMLET. O, but she'll keep her word.

KING. Have you heard the argument? Is there no offence in't?

HAMLET. No, no, they do but jest – poison in jest. No offence i'th' world.

KING. What do you call the play?

HAMLET. The Mousetrap – marry, how tropically! This play is the image of a murder done in Vienna – Gonzago is the Duke's name, his wife Baptista – you shall see anon. 'Tis a knavish piece of work, but what o' that? Your Majesty, and we that have free souls, it touches us not. Let the galled jade wince, our withers are unwrung.

(Enter Lucianus.)

This is one Lucianus, nephew to the King.

OPHELIA. You are as good as a chorus, my lord.

HAMLET. I could interpret between you and your love if I could see the puppets dallying.

OPHELIA. You are keen, my lord, you are keen.

HAMLET. It would cost you a groaning to take off my edge.

OPHELIA. Still better, and worse.

HAMLET. So you mis-take your husbands. – Begin, murderer. Leave thy damnable faces and begin. Come, the croaking raven doth bellow for revenge.

LUCIANUS.
Thoughts black, hands apt, drugs fit, and time agreeing,
Confederate season, else no creature seeing,
Thou mixture rank, of midnight weeds collected,
With Hecate's ban thrice blasted, thrice infected,
Thy natural magic and dire property
On wholesome life usurps immediately.

(Pours the poison in the sleeper's ears.)

HAMLET. A poisons him i'th' garden for his estate. His name's Gonzago. The story is extant, and written in very choice Italian. You shall see anon how the murderer gets the love of Gonzago's wife.

OPHELIA. The King rises.

HAMLET. What, frighted with false fire?

QUEEN. How fares my lord?

POLONIUS. Give o'er the play.

KING. Give me some light. Away.

POLONIUS. Lights, lights, lights.

(Exeunt all but Hamlet and Horatio.)

HAMLET.
Why, let the strucken deer go weep,
The hart ungalled play;
For some must watch while some must sleep,
Thus runs the world away.

Would not this, sir, and a forest of feathers, if the rest of my fortunes turn Turk with me, with Provincial roses on my razed shoes, get me a fellowship in a cry of players?

HORATIO. Half a share.

HAMLET. A whole one, I.
For thou dost know, O Damon dear,
This realm dismantled was
Of Jove himself, and now reigns here
A very, very – pajock.

HORATIO. You might have rhymed.

HAMLET. O good Horatio, I'll take the ghost's word for a thousand pound. Didst perceive?

HORATIO. Very well, my lord.

HAMLET. Upon the talk of the poisoning?

HORATIO. I did very well note him.

HAMLET. Ah ha! Come, some music; come, the recorders.
For if the King like not the comedy,
Why then, belike he likes it not, perdie.

Come, some music.

(Enter Rosencrantz and Guildenstern.)

GUILDENSTERN. Good my lord, vouchsafe me a word with you.

HAMLET. Sir, a whole history.

GUILDENSTERN. The King, sir –

HAMLET. Ay, sir, what of him?

GUILDENSTERN. Is in his retirement marvellous distempered.

HAMLET. With drink, sir?

GUILDENSTERN. No, my lord, with choler.

HAMLET. Your wisdom should show itself more richer to signify this to the doctor, for for me to put him to his purgation would perhaps plunge him into more choler.

GUILDENSTERN. Good my lord, put your discourse into some frame, and start not so wildly from my affair.

HAMLET. I am tame, sir. Pronounce.

GUILDENSTERN. The Queen your mother, in most great affliction of spirit, hath sent me to you.

HAMLET. You are welcome.

GUILDENSTERN. Nay, good my lord, this courtesy is not of the right breed. If it shall please you to make me a wholesome answer, I will do your mother's commandment; if not, your pardon and my return shall be the end of my business.

HAMLET. Sir, I cannot.

ROSENCRANTZ. What, my lord?

HAMLET. Make you a wholesome answer. My wit's diseased. But sir, such answer as I can make, you shall command – or rather, as you say, my mother. Therefore no more, but to the matter. My mother, you say –

ROSENCRANTZ. Then thus she says: your behaviour hath struck her into amazement and admiration.

HAMLET. O wonderful son, that can so stonish a mother! But is there no sequel at the heels of this mother's admiration? Impart.

ROSENCRANTZ. She desires to speak with you in her closet ere you go to bed.

HAMLET. We shall obey, were she ten times our mother. Have you any further trade with us?

ROSENCRANTZ. My lord, you once did love me.

HAMLET. And do still, by these pickers and stealers.

ROSENCRANTZ. Good my lord, what is your cause of distemper? You do surely bar the door upon your own liberty if you deny your griefs to your friend.

HAMLET. Sir, I lack advancement.

ROSENCRANTZ. How can that be, when you have the voice of the King himself for your succession in Denmark?

HAMLET. Ay, sir, but while the grass grows – the proverb is something musty.

(Enter the Players with recorders.)

O, the recorders. Let me see one. – To withdraw with you, why do you go about to recover the wind of me, as if you would drive me into a toil?

GUILDENSTERN. O my lord, if my duty be too bold, my love is too unmannerly.

HAMLET. I do not well understand that. Will you play upon this pipe?

GUILDENSTERN. My lord, I cannot.

HAMLET. I pray you.

GUILDENSTERN. Believe me, I cannot.

HAMLET. I do beseech you.

GUILDENSTERN. I know no touch of it, my lord.

HAMLET. It is as easy as lying. Govern these ventages with your fingers and thumb, give it breath with your mouth, and it will discourse most eloquent music. Look you, these are the stops.

GUILDENSTERN. But these cannot I command to any utterance of harmony. I have not the skill.

HAMLET. Why, look you now, how unworthy a thing you make of me. You would play upon me, you would seem to know my stops, you would pluck out the heart of my mystery, you would sound me from my lowest note to the top of my compass; and there is much music, excellent voice, in this little organ, yet cannot you make it speak. 'Sblood, do you think I am easier to be played on than a pipe? Call me what instrument you will, though you fret me, you cannot play upon me.

(Enter Polonius.)

God bless you, sir.

POLONIUS. My lord, the Queen would speak with you, and presently.

HAMLET. Do you see yonder cloud that's almost in shape of a camel?

POLONIUS. By th' mass and 'tis – like a camel indeed.

HAMLET. Methinks it is like a weasel.

POLONIUS. It is backed like a weasel.

HAMLET. Or like a whale.

POLONIUS. Very like a whale.

HAMLET. Then I will come to my mother by and by. – *(Aside)* They fool me to the top of my bent. – I will come by and by.

POLONIUS. I will say so. *(Exit.)*

HAMLET. "By and by" is easily said. – Leave me, friends.
(Exeunt all but Hamlet.)
'Tis now the very witching time of night,
When churchyards yawn and hell itself breathes out
Contagion to this world. Now could I drink hot blood,
And do such bitter business as the day
Would quake to look on. Soft, now to my mother.
O heart, lose not thy nature. Let not ever
The soul of Nero enter this firm bosom;
Let me be cruel, not unnatural.
I will speak daggers to her, but use none.
My tongue and soul in this be hypocrites:
How in my words somever she be shent,
To give them seals never my soul consent. *(Exit.)*

SCENE III

Enter King, Rosencrantz, and Guildenstern.

KING. I like him not, nor stands it safe with us
To let his madness range. Therefore prepare you.
I your commission will forthwith dispatch,
And he to England shall along with you.
The terms of our estate may not endure
Hazard so near us as doth hourly grow
Out of his brows.
GUILDENSTERN. We will ourselves provide.
Most holy and religious fear it is
To keep those many many bodies safe
That live and feed upon your Majesty.
ROSENCRANTZ. The single and peculiar life is bound
With all the strength and armour of the mind
To keep itself from noyance; but much more
That spirit upon whose weal depends and rests
The lives of many. The cess of majesty
Dies not alone, but like a gulf doth draw
What's near it with it. Or it is a massy wheel
Fix'd on the summit of the highest mount,
To whose huge spokes ten thousand lesser things
Are mortis'd and adjoin'd, which when it falls,
Each small annexment, petty consequence,
Attends the boist'rous ruin. Never alone

Did the King sigh, but with a general groan.
KING. Arm you, I pray you, to this speedy voyage,
For we will fetters put about this fear
Which now goes too free-footed.
ROSENCRANTZ. We will haste us.
(Exeunt Rosencrantz and Guildenstern.)
(Enter Polonius.)
POLONIUS. My lord, he's going to his mother's closet.
Behind the arras I'll convey myself
To hear the process. I'll warrant she'll tax him home,
And as you said – and wisely was it said –
'Tis meet that some more audience than a mother,
Since nature makes them partial, should o'erhear
The speech of vantage. Fare you well, my liege.
I'll call upon you ere you go to bed,
And tell you what I know.
KING. Thanks, dear my lord.
(Exit Polonius.)
O, my offence is rank, it smells to heaven;
It hath the primal eldest curse upon't –
A brother's murder. Pray can I not,
Though inclination be as sharp as will,
My stronger guilt defeats my strong intent,
And, like a man to double business bound,
I stand in pause where I shall first begin,
And both neglect. What if this cursed hand
Were thicker than itself with brother's blood,
Is there not rain enough in the sweet heavens
To wash it white as snow? Whereto serves mercy
But to confront the visage of offence?
And what's in prayer but this twofold force,
To be forestalled ere we come to fall
Or pardon'd being down? Then I'll look up.
My fault is past – but O, what form of prayer
Can serve my turn? "Forgive me my foul murder?"
That cannot be, since I am still possess'd
Of those effects for which I did the murder –
My crown, mine own ambition, and my queen.
May one be pardon'd and retain th'offence?
In the corrupted currents of this world
Offence's gilded hand may shove by justice,
And oft 'tis seen the wicked prize itself
Buys out the law. But 'tis not so above:

There is no shuffling, there the action lies
In his true nature, and we ourselves compell'd
Even to the teeth and forehead of our faults
To give in evidence. What then? What rests?
Try what repentance can. What can it not?
Yet what can it, when one cannot repent?
O wretched state! O bosom black as death!
O limed soul, that struggling to be free
Art more engag'd! Help, angels! Make assay.
Bow, stubborn knees; and heart with strings of steel,
Be soft as sinews of the new-born babe.
All may be well. *(He kneels.)*

(Enter Hamlet.)

HAMLET. Now might I do it pat, now a is a-praying.
And now I'll do't. *(Draws his sword.)*
And so a goes to heaven;
And so am I reveng'd. That would be scann'd:
A villain kills my father, and for that
I, his sole son, do this same villain send
To heaven.
Why, this is hire and salary, not revenge.
A took my father grossly, full of bread,
With all his crimes broad blown, as flush as May;
And how his audit stands who knows save heaven?
But in our circumstance and course of thought
'Tis heavy with him. And am I then reveng'd,
To take him in the purging of his soul,
When he is fit and season'd for his passage?
No.
Up, sword, and know thou a more horrid hent:
When he is drunk asleep, or in his rage,
Or in th'incestuous pleasure of his bed,
At game a-swearing, or about some act
That has no relish of salvation in't,
Then trip him, that his heels may kick at heaven
And that his soul may be as damn'd and black
As hell, whereto it goes. My mother stays.
This physic but prolongs thy sickly days. *(Exit)*

KING. My words fly up, my thoughts remain below.
Words without thoughts never to heaven go.

(Exit)

SCENE IV

Enter Queen and Polonius.

POLONIUS. A will come straight. Look you lay home to him,
Tell him his pranks have been too broad to bear with
And that your Grace hath screen'd and stood between
Much heat and him. I'll silence me even here.
Pray you be round.
QUEEN. I'll war'nt you, fear me not.
Withdraw, I hear him coming. *(Polonius hides behind the arras.)*
(Enter Hamlet.)
HAMLET. Now, mother, what's the matter?
QUEEN. Hamlet, thou hast thy father much offended.
HAMLET. Mother, you have my father much offended.
QUEEN. Come, come, you answer with an idle tongue.
HAMLET. Go, go, you question with a wicked tongue.
QUEEN. Why, how now, Hamlet?
HAMLET. What's the matter now?
QUEEN. Have you forgot me?
HAMLET. No, by the rood, not so.
You are the Queen, your husband's brother's wife,
And, would it were not so, you are my mother.
QUEEN. Nay, then I'll set those to you that can speak.
HAMLET. Come, come, and sit you down, you shall not budge.
You go not till I set you up a glass
Where you may see the inmost part of you.
QUEEN. What wilt thou do? Thou wilt not murder me?
Help, ho!
POLONIUS *(behind the arras).* What ho! Help!
HAMLET. How now? A rat! Dead for a ducat, dead.
(Thrusts his rapier through the arras.)
POLONIUS *(behind).* O, I am slain.
QUEEN. O me, what hast thou done?
HAMLET. Nay, I know not,
Is it the King? *(Lifts up the arras and discovers Polonius, dead.)*
QUEEN. O what a rash and bloody deed is this!
HAMLET. A bloody deed. Almost as bad, good mother,
As kill a king and marry with his brother.
QUEEN. As kill a king?
HAMLET. Ay, lady, it was my word. –
Thou wretched, rash, intruding fool, farewell.
I took thee for thy better. Take thy fortune:

Thou find'st to be too busy is some danger. –
Leave wringing of your hands. Peace, sit you down,
And let me wring your heart; for so I shall
If it be made of penetrable stuff,
If damned custom have not braz'd it so,
That it be proof and bulwark against sense.

QUEEN. What have I done, that thou dar'st wag thy tongue
In noise so rude against me?

HAMLET. Such an act
That blurs the grace and blush of modesty,
Calls virtue hypocrite, takes off the rose
From the fair forehead of an innocent love
And sets a blister there, makes marriage vows
As false as dicers' oaths – O, such a deed
As from the body of contraction plucks
The very soul, and sweet religion makes
A rhapsody of words. Heaven's face does glow
O'er this solidity and compound mass
With tristful visage, as against the doom,
Is thought-sick at the act.

QUEEN. Ay me, what act
That roars so loud and thunders in the index?

HAMLET. Look here upon this picture, and on this,
The counterfeit presentment of two brothers.
See what a grace was seated on this brow,
Hyperion's curls, the front of Jove himself,
An eye like Mars to threaten and command,
A station like the herald Mercury
New-lighted on a heaven-kissing hill,
A combination and a form indeed
Where every god did seem to set his seal
To give the world assurance of a man.
This was your husband. Look you now what follows.
Here is your husband, like a mildew'd ear
Blasting his wholesome brother. Have you eyes?
Could you on this fair mountain leave to feed
And batten on this moor? Ha, have you eyes?
You cannot call it love; for at your age
The heyday in the blood is tame, it's humble,
And waits upon the judgment, and what judgment
Would step from this to this? Sense sure you have,
Else could you not have motion; but sure that sense
Is apoplex'd, for madness would not err

Nor sense to ecstasy was ne'er so thrall'd
But it reserv'd some quantity of choice
To serve in such a difference. What devil was't
That thus hath cozen'd you at hoodman-blind?
Eyes without feeling, feeling without sight,
Ears without hands or eyes, smelling sans all,
Or but a sickly part of one true sense
Could not so mope. O shame, where is thy blush?
Rebellious hell,
If thou canst mutine in a matron's bones,
To flaming youth let virtue be as wax
And melt in her own fire; proclaim no shame
When the compulsive ardour gives the charge,
Since frost itself as actively doth burn
And reason panders will.
QUEEN. O Hamlet, speak no more.
Thou turn'st my eyes into my very soul,
And there I see such black and grained spots
As will not leave their tinct.
HAMLET. Nay, but to live
In the rank sweat of an enseamed bed,
Stew'd in corruption, honeying and making love
Over the nasty sty!
QUEEN. O speak to me no more.
These words like daggers enter in my ears.
No more, sweet Hamlet.
HAMLET. A murderer and a villain,
A slave that is not twentieth part the tithe
Of your precedent lord, a vice of kings,
A cutpurse of the empire and the rule,
That from a shelf the precious diadem stole
And put it in his pocket –
QUEEN. No more.
HAMLET. A king of shreds and patches –
(Enter Ghost.)
Save me and hover o'er me with your wings,
You heavenly guards! What would your gracious figure?
QUEEN. Alas, he's mad.
HAMLET. Do you not come your tardy son to chide,
That, laps'd in time and passion, lets go by
Th'important acting of your dread command?
O say.
GHOST. Do not forget. This visitation

Is but to whet thy almost blunted purpose.
But look, amazement on thy mother sits.
O step between her and her fighting soul.
Conceit in weakest bodies strongest works.
Speak to her, Hamlet.
HAMLET. How is it with you, lady?
QUEEN. Alas, how is't with you,
That you do bend your eye on vacancy,
And with th'incorporal air do hold discourse?
Forth at your eyes your spirits wildly peep,
And, as the sleeping soldiers in th'alarm,
Your bedded hair, like life in excrements,
Start up and stand an end. O gentle son,
Upon the heat and flame of thy distemper
Sprinkle cool patience. Whereon do you look?
HAMLET. On him, on him. Look you how pale he glares.
His form and cause conjoin'd, preaching to stones,
Would make them capable. – Do not look upon me,
Lest with this piteous action you convert
My stern effects. Then what I have to do
Will want true colour – tears perchance for blood.
QUEEN. To whom do you speak this?
HAMLET. Do you see nothing there?
QUEEN. Nothing at all; yet all that is I see.
HAMLET. Nor did you nothing hear?
QUEEN. No, nothing but ourselves.
HAMLET. Why, look you there, look how it steals away.
My father, in his habit as he liv'd!
Look where he goes even now out at the portal. *(Exit Ghost.)*
QUEEN. This is the very coinage of your brain.
This bodiless creation ecstasy
Is very cunning in.
HAMLET. My pulse as yours doth temperately keep time,
And makes as healthful music. It is not madness
That I have utter'd. Bring me to the test,
And I the matter will re-word, which madness.
Would gambol from. Mother, for love of grace,
Lay not that flattering unction to your soul,
That not your trespass but my madness speaks.
It will but skin and film the ulcerous place,
Whiles rank corruption, mining all within,
Infects unseen. Confess yourself to heaven,
Repent what's past, avoid what is to come;

And do not spread the compost on the weeds
To make them ranker. Forgive me this my virtue;
For in the fatness of these pursy times
Virtue itself of vice must pardon beg,
Yea, curb and woo for leave to do him good.
QUEEN. O Hamlet, thou hast cleft my heart in twain.
HAMLET. O throw away the worser part of it
And live the purer with the other half.
Good night. But go not to my uncle's bed.
Assume a virtue if you have it not.
That monster, custom, who all sense doth eat
Of habits evil, is angel yet in this,
That to the use of actions fair and good
He likewise gives a frock or livery
That aptly is put on. Refrain tonight,
And that shall lend a kind of easiness
To the next abstinence, the next more easy;
For use almost can change the stamp of nature,
And either (lodge) the devil or throw him out
With wondrous potency. Once more, good night,
And when you are desirous to be blest,
I'll blessing beg of you. For this same lord
I do repent; but heaven hath pleas'd it so,
To punish me with this and this with me,
That I must be their scourge and minister.
I will bestow him, and will answer well
The death I gave him. So, again, good night.
I must be cruel only to be kind.
This bad begins, and worse remains behind.
One word more, good lady.
QUEEN. What shall I do?
HAMLET. Not this, by no means, that I bid you do:
Let the bloat King tempt you again to bed,
Pinch wanton on your cheek, call you his mouse,
And let him, for a pair of reechy kisses,
Or paddling in your neck with his damn'd fingers,
Make you to ravel all this matter out
That I essentially am not in madness,
But mad in craft. 'Twere good you let him know,
For who that's but a queen, fair, sober, wise,
Would from a paddock, from a bat, a gib,
Such dear concernings hide? Who would do so?
No, in despite of sense and secrecy,

Unpeg the basket on the house's top,
Let the birds fly, and like the famous ape,
To try conclusions, in the basket creep,
And break your own neck down.

QUEEN. Be thou assur'd, if words be made of breath,
And breath of life, I have no life to breathe
What thou hast said to me.

HAMLET. I must to England, you know that?

QUEEN. Alack,
I had forgot. 'Tis so concluded on.

HAMLET. There's letters seal'd, and my two schoolfellows,
Whom I will trust as I will adders fang'd –
They bear the mandate, they must sweep my way
And marshal me to knavery. Let it work;
For 'tis the sport to have the enginer
Hoist with his own petard, and't shall go hard
But I will delve one yard below their mines
And blow them at the moon. O, 'tis most sweet
When in one line two crafts directly meet.
This man shall set me packing.
I'll lug the guts into the neighbour room.
Mother, good night indeed. This counsellor
Is now most still, most secret, and most grave,
Who was in life a foolish prating knave.
Come, sir, to draw toward an end with you.
Good night, mother.

(Exit lugging in Polonius. The Queen remains.)

ACT IV

SCENE I

To the Queen, enter King, with Rosencrantz and Guildenstern.

KING. There's matter in these sighs, these profound heaves,
You must translate. 'Tis fit we understand them.
Where is your son?
QUEEN. Bestow this place on us a little while.
(Exeunt Rosencrantz and Guildenstern.)
Ah, mine own lord, what have I seen tonight!
KING. What, Gertrude, how does Hamlet?
QUEEN. Mad as the sea and wind when both contend
Which is the mightier. In his lawless fit,
Behind the arras hearing something stir,
Whips out his rapier, cries "A rat, a rat",
And in this brainish apprehension kills
The unseen good old man.
KING. O heavy deed!
It had been so with us had we been there.
His liberty is full of threats to all –
To you yourself, to us, to everyone.
Alas, how shall this bloody deed be answer'd?
It will be laid to us, whose providence
Should have kept short, restrain'd, and out of haunt
This mad young man. But so much was our love,
We would not understand what was most fit,
But like the owner of a foul disease,
To keep it from divulging, let it feed
Even on the pith of life. Where is he gone?
QUEEN. To draw apart the body he hath kill'd,
O'er whom – his very madness, like some ore
Among a mineral of metals base,
Shows itself pure – a weeps for what is done.
KING. O Gertrude, come away.
The sun no sooner shall the mountains touch
But we will ship him hence; and this vile deed
We must with all our majesty and skill
Both countenance and excuse. – Ho, Guildenstern!
(Enter Rosencrantz and Guildenstern.)
Friends both, go join you with some further aid.

Hamlet in madness hath Polonius slain,
And from his mother's closet hath he dragg'd him.
Go seek him out – speak fair – and bring the body
Into the chapel. I pray you haste in this.
(Exeunt Rosencrantz and Guildenstern.)
Come, Gertrude, we'll call up our wisest friends,
And let them know both what we mean to do
And what's untimely done. (So envious slander),
Whose whisper o'er the world's diameter,
As level as the cannon to his blank,
Transports his poison'd shot, may miss our name
And hit the woundless air. O come away,
My soul is full of discord and dismay.
(Exeunt.)

SCENE II

Enter Hamlet.

HAMLET. Safely stowed. *(Calling within.)*
But soft, what noise? Who calls on Hamlet? O, here they come.
(Enter Rosencrantz, Guildenstern, and Others.)

ROSENCRANTZ. What have you done, my lord, with the dead body?

HAMLET. Compounded it with dust, whereto 'tis kin.

ROSENCRANTZ. Tell us where 'tis, that we may take it thence and bear it to the chapel.

HAMLET. Do not believe it.

ROSENCRANTZ. Believe what?

HAMLET. That I can keep your counsel and not mine own. Besides, to be demanded of a sponge – what replication should be made by the son of a king?

ROSENCRANTZ. Take you me for a sponge, my lord?

HAMLET. Ay, sir, that soaks up the King's countenance, his rewards, his authorities. But such officers do the King best service in the end: he keeps them, like an ape, in the corner of his jaw – first mouthed, to be last swallowed. When he needs what you have gleaned, it is but squeezing you and, sponge, you shall be dry again.

ROSENCRANTZ. I understand you not, my lord.

HAMLET. I am glad of it. A knavish speech sleeps in a foolish ear.

ROSENCRANTZ. My lord, you must tell us where the body is and go with us to the King.

HAMLET. The body is with the King, but the King is not with the body. The King is a thing –
GUILDENSTERN. A thing, my lord?
HAMLET. Of nothing. Bring me to him. *(Exeunt.)*

SCENE III

Enter King and two or three Lords.

KING. I have sent to seek him and to find the body.
How dangerous is it that this man goes loose!
Yet must not we put the strong law on him:
He's lov'd of the distracted multitude,
Who like not in their judgment but their eyes,
And where 'tis so, th'offender's scourge is weigh'd,
But never the offence. To bear all smooth and even,
This sudden sending him away must seem
Deliberate pause. Diseases desperate grown
By desperate appliance are reliev'd,
Or not at all.
(Enter Rosencrantz, Guildenstern, and Others.)
How now, what hath befall'n?
ROSENCRANTZ. Where the dead body is bestow'd, my lord,
We cannot get from him.
KING. But where is he?
ROSENCRANTZ.
Without, my lord, guarded, to know your pleasure.
KING. Bring him before us.
ROSENCRANTZ. Ho! Bring in the lord.
(Enter Hamlet with Guards.)
KING. Now, Hamlet, where's Polonius?
HAMLET. At supper.
KING. At supper? Where?
HAMLET. Not where he eats, but where a is eaten. A certain convocation of politic worms are e'en at him. Your worm is your only emperor for diet: we fat all creatures else to fat us, and we fat ourselves for maggots. Your fat king and your lean beggar is but variable service – two dishes, but to one table. That's the end.
KING. Alas, alas.
HAMLET. A man may fish with the worm that hath eat of a king, and eat of the fish that hath fed of that worm.

KING. What dost thou mean by this?

HAMLET. Nothing but to show you how a king may go a progress through the guts of a beggar.

KING. Where is Polonius?

HAMLET. In heaven. Send thither to see. If your messenger find him not there, seek him i'th'other place yourself. But if indeed you find him not within this month, you shall nose him as you go up the stairs into the lobby.

KING *(To some Attendants).* Go seek him there.

HAMLET. A will stay till you come. *(Exeunt Attendants.)*

KING. Hamlet, this deed, for thine especial safety –
Which we do tender, as we dearly grieve
For that which thou hast done – must send thee hence
With fiery quickness. Therefore prepare thyself.
The bark is ready, and the wind at help,
Th'associates tend, and everything is bent
For England.

HAMLET. For England?

KING. Ay, Hamlet.

HAMLET. Good.

KING. So is it, if thou knew'st our purposes.

HAMLET. I see a cherub that sees them. But come, for England. Farewell, dear mother.

KING. Thy loving father, Hamlet.

HAMLET. My mother. Father and mother is man and wife, man and wife is one flesh; so my mother. Come, for England. *(Exit.)*

KING. Follow him at foot. Tempt him with speed aboard,
Delay it not – I'll have him hence tonight.
Away, for everything is seal'd and done
That else leans on th'affair. Pray you make haste.
(Exeunt all but the King.)
And England, if my love thou hold'st at aught –
As my great power thereof may give thee sense,
Since yet thy cicatrice looks raw and red
After the Danish sword, and thy free awe
Pays homage to us – thou mayst not coldly set
Our sovereign process, which imports at full,
By letters congruing to that effect,
The present death of Hamlet. Do it, England;
For like the hectic in my blood he rages,
And thou must cure me. Till I know 'tis done,
Howe'er my haps, my joys were ne'er begun. *(Exit.)*

SCENE IV

Enter Fortinbras with his Army, marching over the stage.

FORTINBRAS. Go, captain, from me greet the Danish king.
Tell him that by his licence Fortinbras
Craves the conveyance of a promis'd march
Over his kingdom. You know the rendezvous.
If that his Majesty would aught with us,
We shall express our duty in his eye;
And let him know so.
CAPTAIN. I will do't, my lord.
FORTINBRAS. Go softly on. *(Exeunt all but the Captain.)*

(Enter Hamlet, Rosencrantz, Guildenstern, and Others.)

HAMLET. Good sir, whose powers are these?
CAPTAIN. They are of Norway, sir.
HAMLET. How purpos'd, sir, I pray you?
CAPTAIN. Against some part of Poland.
HAMLET. Who commands them, sir?
CAPTAIN. The nephew to old Norway, Fortinbras.
HAMLET. Goes it against the main of Poland, sir,
Or for some frontier?
CAPTAIN. Truly to speak, and with no addition,
We go to gain a little patch of ground
That hath in it no profit but the name.
To pay five ducats – five – I would not farm it;
Nor will it yield to Norway or the Pole
A ranker rate should it be sold in fee.
HAMLET. Why, then the Polack never will defend it.
CAPTAIN. Yes, it is already garrison'd.
HAMLET. Two thousand souls and twenty thousand ducats
Will not debate the question of this straw!
This is th'impostume of much wealth and peace,
That inward breaks, and shows no cause without
Why the man dies. I humbly thank you, sir.
CAPTAIN. God buy you, sir. *(Exit.)*
ROSENCRANTZ. Will't please you go, my lord?
HAMLET. I'll be with you straight. Go a little before.
(Exeunt all but Hamlet.)
How all occasions do inform against me,
And spur my dull revenge. What is a man
If his chief good and market of his time

Be but to sleep and feed? A beast, no more.
Sure he that made us with such large discourse,
Looking before and after, gave us not
That capability and godlike reason
To fust in us unus'd. Now whether it be
Bestial oblivion, or some craven scruple
Of thinking too precisely on th'event –
A thought which, quarter'd, hath but one part wisdom
And ever three parts coward – I do not know
Why yet I live to say this thing's to do,
Sith I have cause, and will, and strength, and means
To do't. Examples gross as earth exhort me,
Witness this army of such mass and charge,
Led by a delicate and tender prince,
Whose spirit, with divine ambition puff'd,
Makes mouths at the invisible event,
Exposing what is mortal and unsure
To all that fortune, death, and danger dare,
Even for an eggshell. Rightly to be great
Is not to stir without great argument,
But greatly to find quarrel in a straw
When honour's at the stake. How stand I then,
That have a father kill'd, a mother stain'd,
Excitements of my reason and my blood,
And let all sleep, while to my shame I see
The imminent death of twenty thousand men
That, for a fantasy and trick of fame,
Go to their graves like beds, fight for a plot
Whereon the numbers cannot try the cause,
Which is not tomb enough and continent
To hide the slain? O, from this time forth
My thoughts be bloody or be nothing worth. *(Exit.)*

SCENE V

Enter Queen, Horatio, and a Gentleman.

QUEEN. I will not speak with her.
GENTLEMAN. She is importunate,
Indeed distract. Her mood will needs be pitied.
QUEEN. What would she have?
GENTLEMAN. She speaks much of her father, says she hears

There's tricks i'th' world, and hems, and beats her heart,
Spurns enviously at straws, speaks things in doubt
That carry but half sense. Her speech is nothing,
Yet the unshaped use of it doth move
The hearers to collection. They aim at it,
And botch the words up fit to their own thoughts,
Which, as her winks and nods and gestures yield them,
Indeed would make one think there might be thought,
Though nothing sure, yet much unhappily.

HORATIO.
'Twere good she were spoken with, for she may strew
Dangerous conjectures in ill-breeding minds.

QUEEN. Let her come in. *(Exit Gentleman.)*
(Aside) To my sick soul, as sin's true nature is,
Each toy seems prologue to some great amiss.
So full of artless jealousy is guilt,
It spills itself in fearing to be spilt.

(Enter Ophelia.)

OPHELIA. Where is the beauteous Majesty of Denmark?

QUEEN. How now, Ophelia?

OPHELIA *(sings).*
How should I your true love know
From another one?
By his cockle hat and staff
And his sandal shoon.

QUEEN. Alas, sweet lady, what imports this song?

OPHELIA. Say you? Nay, pray you mark.
(sings) He is dead and gone, lady,
He is dead and gone,
At his head a grass-green turf,
At his heels a stone.
O ho!

QUEEN. Nay, but Ophelia –

OPHELIA. Pray you mark.
(sings) White his shroud as the mountain snow –

(Enter King.)

QUEEN. Alas, look here, my lord.

OPHELIA *(sings).*
Larded with sweet flowers
Which bewept to the grave did not go
With true-love showers.

KING. How do you, pretty lady?

OPHELIA. Well, good dild you. They say the owl was a baker's daughter. Lord, we know what we are, but know not what we may be. God be at your table.

KING. Conceit upon her father.

OPHELIA. Pray let's have no words of this, but when they ask you what it means, say you this.

(sings) Tomorrow is Saint Valentine's day,
All in the morning betime,
And I a maid at your window,
To be your Valentine.
Then up he rose, and donn'd his clo'es,
And dupp'd the chamber door,
Let in the maid that out a maid
Never departed more.

KING. Pretty Ophelia –

OPHELIA. Indeed, without an oath, I'll make an end on't.

By Gis and by Saint Charity,
Alack and fie for shame,
Young men will do't if they come to't –
By Cock, they are to blame.
Quoth she, "Before you tumbled me,
You promis'd me to wed."
He answers,
"So would I a done, by yonder sun,
And thou hadst not come to my bed."

KING. How long hath she been thus?

OPHELIA. I hope all will be well. We must be patient. But I cannot choose but weep to think they would lay him i'th' cold ground. My brother shall know of it. And so I thank you for your good counsel. Come, my coach. Good night, ladies, good night. Sweet ladies, good night, good night. *(Exit.)*

KING. Follow her close; give her good watch, I pray you.
(Exit Horatio.)

O, this is the poison of deep grief: it springs
All from her father's death. And now behold –
O Gertrude, Gertrude,
When sorrows come, they come not single spies,
But in battalions. First, her father slain;
Next, your son gone, and he most violent author
Of his own just remove; the people muddied,
Thick and unwholesome in their thoughts and whispers
For good Polonius' death – and we have done but greenly
In hugger-mugger to inter him; poor Ophelia
Divided from herself and her fair judgment,

Without the which we are pictures, or mere beasts;
Last, and as much containing as all these,
Her brother is in secret come from France,
Feeds on this wonder, keeps himself in clouds,
And wants not buzzers to infect his ear
With pestilent speeches of his father's death,
Wherein necessity, of matter beggar'd,
Will nothing stick our person to arraign
In ear and ear. O my dear Gertrude, this,
Like to a murd'ring-piece, in many places
Gives me superfluous death. *(A noise within.)*
Attend!
Where is my Switzers? Let them guard the door.
(Enter a Messenger.)
What is the matter?
MESSENGER. Save yourself, my lord.
The ocean, overpeering of his list,
Eats not the flats with more impetuous haste
Than young Laertes, in a riotous head,
O'erbears your officers. The rabble call him lord,
And, as the world were now but to begin,
Antiquity forgot, custom not known –
The ratifiers and props of every word –
They cry, "Choose we! Laertes shall be king."
Caps, hands, and tongues applaud it to the clouds,
"Laertes shall be king, Laertes king."
QUEEN. How cheerfully on the false trail they cry.
O, this is counter, you false Danish dogs. *(A noise within.)*
KING. The doors are broke.
(Enter Laertes with Followers.)
LAERTES. Where is this king? – Sirs, stand you all without.
FOLLOWERS. No, let's come in.
LAERTES. I pray you give me leave.
FOLLOWERS. We will, we will.
LAERTES. I thank you. Keep the door. *(Exeunt Followers.)*
O thou vile king,
Give me my father.
QUEEN *(holding him).* Calmly, good Laertes.
LAERTES. That drop of blood that's calm proclaims me bastard,
Cries cuckold to my father, brands the harlot
Even here between the chaste unsmirched brow
Of my true mother.
KING. What is the cause, Laertes,

That thy rebellion looks so giant-like? –
Let him go, Gertrude. Do not fear our person.
There's such divinity doth hedge a king
That treason can but peep to what it would,
Acts little of his will. – Tell me, Laertes,
Why thou art thus incens'd. – Let him go, Gertrude. –
Speak, man.

LAERTES. Where is my father?

KING. Dead.

QUEEN. But not by him.

KING. Let him demand his fill.

LAERTES. How came he dead? I'll not be juggled with.
To hell, allegiance! Vows to the blackest devil!
Conscience and grace, to the profoundest pit!
I dare damnation. To this point I stand,
That both the worlds I give to negligence,
Let come what comes, only I'll be reveng'd
Most throughly for my father.

KING. Who shall stay you?

LAERTES. My will, not all the world's.
And for my means, I'll husband them so well,
They shall go far with little.

KING. Good Laertes,
If you desire to know the certainty
Of your dear father, is't writ in your revenge
That, swoopstake, you will draw both friend and foe,
Winner and loser?

LAERTES. None but his enemies.

KING. Will you know them then?

LAERTES. To his good friends thus wide I'll ope my arms,
And, like the kind life-rend'ring pelican,
Repast them with my blood.

KING. Why, now you speak
Like a good child and a true gentleman.
That I am guiltless of your father's death
And am most sensibly in grief for it,
It shall as level to your judgment 'pear
As day does to your eye.

(A noise within. Ophelia is heard singing.)

Let her come in.

LAERTES. How now, what noise is that?

(Enter Ophelia.)

O heat, dry up my brains. Tears seven times salt

Burn out the sense and virtue of mine eye.
By heaven, thy madness shall be paid with weight
Till our scale turn the beam. O rose of May!
Dear maid – kind sister – sweet Ophelia –
O heavens, is't possible a young maid's wits
Should be as mortal as an old man's life?
Nature is fine in love, and where 'tis fine
It sends some precious instance of itself
After the thing it loves.

OPHELIA *(sings).*
They bore him bare-fac'd on the bier,
And in his grave rain'd many a tear –
Fare you well, my dove.

LAERTES. Hadst thou thy wits and didst persuade revenge,
It could not move thus.

OPHELIA. You must sing "A-down a-down", and you "Call him a-down-a". O, how the wheel becomes it! It is the false steward that stole his master's daughter.

LAERTES. This nothing's more than matter.

OPHELIA. There's rosemary, that's for remembrance – pray you, love, remember. And there is pansies, that's for thoughts.

LAERTES. A document in madness: thoughts and remembrance fitted.

OPHELIA. There's fennel for you, and columbines. There's rue for you. And here's some for me. We may call it herb of grace a Sundays. You must wear your rue with a difference. There's a daisy. I would give you some violets, but they withered all when my father died. They say a made a good end.
(sings) For bonny sweet Robin is all my joy.

LAERTES. Thought and affliction, passion, hell itself
She turns to favour and to prettiness.

OPHELIA. And will a not come again?
(sings) And will a not come again?
No, no, he is dead,
Go to thy death-bed,
He never will come again.
His beard was as white as snow,
All flaxen was his poll.
He is gone, he is gone,
And we cast away moan.
God a mercy on his soul.
And of all Christian souls. God buy you. *(Exit)*

LAERTES. Do you see this, O God?

KING. Laertes, I must commune with your grief,
Or you deny me right. Go but apart,
Make choice of whom your wisest friends you will,
And they shall hear and judge 'twixt you and me.
If by direct or by collateral hand
They find us touch'd, we will our kingdom give,
Our crown, our life, and all that we call ours
To you in satisfaction; but if not,
Be you content to lend your patience to us,
And we shall jointly labour with your soul
To give it due content.
LAERTES. Let this be so.
His means of death, his obscure funeral –
No trophy, sword, nor hatchment o'er his bones,
No noble rite, nor formal ostentation –
Cry to be heard, as 'twere from heaven to earth,
That I must call't in question.
KING. So you shall.
And where th'offence is, let the great axe fall.
I pray you go with me. *(Exeunt.)*

SCENE VI

Enter Horatio and a Servant.

HORATIO. What are they that would speak with me?
SERVANT. Seafaring men, sir. They say they have letters for you.
HORATIO. Let them come in. *(Exit Servant.)*
I do not know from what part of the world
I should be greeted, if not from Lord Hamlet.
(Enter Sailors.)
FIRST SAILOR. God bless you, sir.
HORATIO. Let him bless thee too.
FIRST SAILOR. A shall, sir, and please him. There's a letter for you, sir. It came from th'ambassador that was bound for England – if your name be Horatio, as I am let to know it is.

HORATIO *(reads the letter)*. "Horatio, when thou shalt have overlooked this, give these fellows some means to the King. They have letters for him. Ere we were two days old at sea, a pirate of very warlike appointment gave us chase. Finding ourselves too slow of sail, we put on a compelled valour, and in the grapple I boarded them. On the instant they got clear of our ship, so I alone became their prisoner. They have dealt with me like thieves of mercy. But they knew what they did: I am to do a turn for them. Let the King have the letters I have sent, and repair thou to me with as much speed as thou wouldest fly death. I have words to speak in thine ear will make thee dumb; yet are they much too light for the bore of the matter. These good fellows will bring thee where I am. Rosencrantz and Guildenstern hold their course for England; of them I have much to tell thee. Farewell.

He that thou knowest thine,
Hamlet."

Come, I will give you way for these your letters,
And do't the speedier that you may direct me
To him from whom you brought them. *(Exeunt.)*

SCENE VII

Enter King and Laertes.

KING. Now must your conscience my acquittance seal,
And you must put me in your heart for friend,
Sith you have heard, and with a knowing ear,
That he which hath your noble father slain
Pursu'd my life.
LAERTES. It well appears. But tell me
Why you proceeded not against these feats,
So crimeful and so capital in nature,
As by your safety, wisdom, all things else
You mainly were stirr'd up.
KING. O, for two special reasons,
Which may to you perhaps seem much unsinew'd,
But yet to me th'are strong. The Queen his mother
Lives almost by his looks, and for myself –
My virtue or my plague, be it either which –
She is so conjunctive to my life and soul
That, as the star moves not but in his sphere,
I could not but by her. The other motive
Why to a public count I might not go
Is the great love the general gender bear him,
Who, dipping all his faults in their affection,
Work like the spring that turneth wood to stone,
Convert his gyves to graces; so that my arrows,
Too slightly timber'd for so loud a wind,

Would have reverted to my bow again,
But not where I had aim'd them.

LAERTES. And so have I a noble father lost,
A sister driven into desp'rate terms,
Whose worth, if praises may go back again,
Stood challenger on mount of all the age
For her perfections. But my revenge will come.

KING. Break not your sleeps for that. You must not think
That we are made of stuff so flat and dull
That we can let our beard be shook with danger
And think it pastime. You shortly shall hear more.
I lov'd your father, and we love ourself,
And that, I hope, will teach you to imagine –

(Enter a Messenger with letters.)

MESSENGER. These to your Majesty, this to the Queen.

KING. From Hamlet! Who brought them?

MESSENGER. Sailors, my lord, they say. I saw them not.
They were given me by Claudio. He receiv'd them
Of him that brought them.

KING. Laertes, you shall hear them. –
Leave us. *(Exit Messenger.)*
(Reads) "High and mighty, you shall know I am set naked on your kingdom. Tomorrow shall I beg leave to see your kingly eyes, when I shall, first asking your pardon, thereunto recount the occasion of my sudden and more strange return.
Hamlet."
What should this mean? Are all the rest come back?
Or is it some abuse, and no such thing?

LAERTES. Know you the hand?

KING. 'Tis Hamlet's character.
"Naked" –
And in a postscript here he says "Alone".
Can you devise me?

LAERTES. I am lost in it, my lord. But let him come.
It warms the very sickness in my heart
That I shall live and tell him to his teeth,
"Thus diest thou".

KING. If it be so, Laertes –
As how should it be so, how otherwise? –
Will you be rul'd by me?

LAERTES. Ay, my lord,
So you will not o'errule me to a peace.

KING. To thine own peace. If he be now return'd,

As checking at his voyage, and that he means
No more to undertake it, I will work him
To an exploit, now ripe in my device,
Under the which he shall not choose but fall;
And for his death no wind of blame shall breathe,
But even his mother shall uncharge the practice
And call it accident.
LAERTES. My lord, I will be rul'd,
The rather if you could devise it so
That I might be the organ.
KING. It falls right.
You have been talk'd of since your travel much,
And that in Hamlet's hearing, for a quality
Wherein they say you shine. Your sum of parts
Did not together pluck such envy from him
As did that one, and that, in my regard,
Of the unworthiest siege.
LAERTES. What part is that, my lord?
KING. A very ribbon in the cap of youth –
Yet needful too, for youth no less becomes
The light and careless livery that it wears
Than settled age his sables and his weeds
Importing health and graveness. Two months since
Here was a gentleman of Normandy –
I have seen myself, and serv'd against, the French,
And they can well on horseback, but this gallant
Had witchcraft in't. He grew unto his seat,
And to such wondrous doing brought his horse
As had he been incorps'd and demi-natur'd
With the brave beast. So far he topp'd my thought
That I in forgery of shapes and tricks
Come short of what he did.
LAERTES. A Norman was't?
KING. A Norman.
LAERTES. Upon my life, Lamord.
KING. The very same.
LAERTES. I know him well. He is the brooch indeed
And gem of all the nation.
KING. He made confession of you,
And gave you such a masterly report
For art and exercise in your defence,
And for your rapier most especial,
That he cried out 'twould be a sight indeed

If one could match you. The scrimers of their nation
He swore had neither motion, guard, nor eye,
If you oppos'd them. Sir, this report of his
Did Hamlet so envenom with his envy
That he could nothing do but wish and beg
Your sudden coming o'er to play with you.
Now out of this –
LAERTES. What out of this, my lord?
KING. Laertes, was your father dear to you?
Or are you like the painting of a sorrow,
A face without a heart?
LAERTES. Why ask you this?
KING. Not that I think you did not love your father,
But that I know love is begun by time,
And that I see, in passages of proof,
Time qualifies the spark and fire of it.
There lives within the very flame of love
A kind of wick or snuff that will abate it;
And nothing is at a like goodness still,
For goodness, growing to a pleurisy,
Dies in his own too-much. That we would do,
We should do when we would: for this "would" changes
And hath abatements and delays as many
As there are tongues, are hands, are accidents,
And then this "should" is like a spendthrift sigh
That hurts by easing. But to the quick of th'ulcer:
Hamlet comes back; what would you undertake
To show yourself in deed your father's son
More than in words?
LAERTES. To cut his throat i'th' church.
KING. No place indeed should murder sanctuarize;
Revenge should have no bounds. But good Laertes,
Will you do this, keep close within your chamber;
Hamlet, return'd, shall know you are come home;
We'll put on those shall praise your excellence,
And set a double varnish on the fame
The Frenchman gave you, bring you, in fine, together,
And wager o'er your heads. He, being remiss,
Most generous, and free from all contriving,
Will not peruse the foils, so that with ease –
Or with a little shuffling – you may choose
A sword unbated, and in a pass of practice
Requite him for your father.

LAERTES. I will do't.
And for that purpose, I'll anoint my sword.
I bought an unction of a mountebank
So mortal that but dip a knife in it,
Where it draws blood, no cataplasm so rare,
Collected from all simples that have virtue
Under the moon, can save the thing from death
That is but scratch'd withal. I'll touch my point
With this contagion, that if I gall him slightly,
It may be death.
KING. Let's further think of this,
Weigh what convenience both of time and means
May fit us to our shape. If this should fail,
And that our drift look through our bad performance,
'Twere better not essay'd. Therefore this project
Should have a back or second that might hold
If this did blast in proof. Soft, let me see.
We'll make a solemn wager on your cunnings –
I ha't!
When in your motion you are hot and dry –
As make your bouts more violent to that end –
And that he calls for drink, I'll have prepar'd him
A chalice for the nonce, whereon but sipping,
If he by chance escape your venom'd stuck,
Our purpose may hold there. But stay, what noise?
(Enter Queen.)
QUEEN. One woe doth tread upon another's heel,
So fast they follow. Your sister's drown'd, Laertes.
LAERTES. Drown'd? O, where?
QUEEN. There is a willow grows askant the brook
That shows his hoary leaves in the glassy stream.
Therewith fantastic garlands did she make
Of crow-flowers, nettles, daisies, and long purples,
That liberal shepherds give a grosser name,
But our cold maids do dead men's fingers call them.
There on the pendent boughs her crownet weeds
Clamb'ring to hang, an envious sliver broke,
When down her weedy trophies and herself
Fell in the weeping brook. Her clothes spread wide,
And mermaid-like awhile they bore her up,
Which time she chanted snatches of old lauds,
As one incapable of her own distress,
Or like a creature native and indued

Unto that element. But long it could not be
Till that her garments, heavy with their drink,
Pull'd the poor wretch from her melodious lay
To muddy death.

LAERTES. Alas, then she is drown'd.

QUEEN. Drown'd, drown'd.

LAERTES. Too much of water hast thou, poor Ophelia,
And therefore I forbid my tears. But yet
It is our trick; nature her custom holds,
Let shame say what it will. *(Weeps.)* When these are gone,
The woman will be out. Adieu, my lord,
I have a speech o' fire that fain would blaze
But that this folly douts it. *(Exit.)*

KING. Let's follow, Gertrude.
How much I had to do to calm his rage.
Now fear I this will give it start again.
Therefore let's follow. *(Exeunt.)*

ACT V

SCENE I

Enter two Clowns – the Grave-digger and Another.

GRAVE-DIGGER. Is she to be buried in Christian burial, when she wilfully seeks her own salvation?

OTHER GRAVE-DIGGER. I tell thee she is, therefore make her grave straight. The crowner hath sat on her and finds it Christian burial.

GRAVE-DIGGER. How can that be, unless she drowned herself in her own defence?

OTHER GRAVE-DIGGER. Why, 'tis found so.

GRAVE-DIGGER. It must be "se offendendo", it cannot be else. For here lies the point: if I drown myself wittingly, it argues an act, and an act hath three branches – it is to act, to do, to perform; argal, she drowned herself wittingly.

OTHER GRAVE-DIGGER. Nay, but hear you, Goodman Delver –

GRAVE-DIGGER. Give me leave. Here lies the water – good. Here stands the man – good. If the man go to this water and drown himself, it is, will he nill he, he goes, mark you that. But if the water come to him and drown him, he drowns not himself. Argal, he that is not guilty of his own death shortens not his own life.

OTHER GRAVE-DIGGER. But is this law?

GRAVE-DIGGER. Ay, marry is't, crowner's quest law.

OTHER GRAVE-DIGGER. Will you ha' the truth an't? If this had not been a gentlewoman, she should have been buried out o' Christian burial.

GRAVE-DIGGER. Why, there thou say'st. And the more pity that great folk should have countenance in this world to drown or hang themselves more than their even-Christen. Come, my spade. There is no ancient gentlemen but gardeners, ditchers, and gravemakers – they hold up Adam's profession. *(He digs.)*

OTHER GRAVE-DIGGER. Was he a gentleman?

GRAVE-DIGGER. A was the first that ever bore arms.

OTHER GRAVE-DIGGER. Why, he had none.

GRAVE-DIGGER. What, art a heathen? How dost thou understand the Scripture? The Scripture says Adam digged. Could he dig without arms? I'll put another question to thee. If thou answerest me not to the purpose, confess thyself –

OTHER GRAVE-DIGGER. Go to.

GRAVE-DIGGER. What is he that builds stronger than either the mason, the shipwright, or the carpenter?

OTHER GRAVE-DIGGER. The gallows-maker, for that frame outlives a thousand tenants.

GRAVE-DIGGER. I like thy wit well in good faith, the gallows does well. But how does it well? It does well to those that do ill. Now, thou dost ill to say the gallows is built stronger than the church; argal, the gallows may do well to thee. To't again, come.

OTHER GRAVE-DIGGER. Who builds stronger than a mason, a shipwright, or a carpenter?

GRAVE-DIGGER. Ay, tell me that and unyoke.

OTHER GRAVE-DIGGER. Marry, now I can tell.

GRAVE-DIGGER. To't.

OTHER GRAVE-DIGGER. Mass, I cannot tell.

GRAVE-DIGGER. Cudgel thy brains no more about it, for your dull ass will not mend his pace with beating. And when you are asked this question next, say "A grave-maker". The houses he makes lasts till doomsday. Go, get thee to Yaughan; fetch me a stoup of liquor.

(Exit the Other Clown. The Grave-digger continues digging.)

(Sings) In youth when I did love, did love,
Methought it was very sweet:
To contract – O – the time for – a – my behove,
O methought there – a – was nothing – a – meet.

(While he is singing, enter Hamlet and Horatio.)

HAMLET. Has this fellow no feeling of his business a sings in grave-making?

HORATIO. Custom hath made it in him a property of easiness.

HAMLET. 'Tis e'en so, the hand of little employment hath the daintier sense.

GRAVE-DIGGER *(sings)*.
But age with his stealing steps
Hath claw'd me in his clutch,
And hath shipp'd me intil the land,
As if I had never been such. *(He throws up a skull.)*

HAMLET. That skull had a tongue in it, and could sing once. How the knave jowls it to th' ground, as if 'twere Cain's jawbone, that did the first murder. This might be the pate of a politician which this ass now o'er-offices, one that would circumvent God, might it not?

HORATIO. It might, my lord.

HAMLET. Or of a courtier, which could say, "Good morrow,

sweet lord. How dost thou, sweet lord?" This might be my Lord Such-a-one, that praised my Lord Such-a-one's horse when a meant to beg it, might it not?

HORATIO. Ay, my lord.

HAMLET. Why, e'en so, and now my Lady Worm's, chopless, and knocked about the mazard with a sexton's spade. Here's fine revolution and we had the trick to see't. Did these bones cost no more the breeding but to play at loggets with 'em? Mine ache to think on't.

GRAVE-DIGGER *(sings).*

A pickaxe and a spade, a spade,
For and a shrouding-sheet,
O a pit of clay for to be made
For such a guest is meet. *(Throws up another skull.)*

HAMLET. There's another. Why, may not that be the skull of a lawyer? Where be his quiddities now, his quillities, his cases, his tenures, and his tricks? Why does he suffer this mad knave now to knock him about the sconce with a dirty shovel, and will not tell him of his action of battery? Hum, this fellow might be in's time a great buyer of land, with his statutes, his recognizances, his fines, his double vouchers, his recoveries. Is this the fine of his fines and the recovery of his recoveries, to have his fine pate full of fine dirt? Will his vouchers vouch him no more of his purchases, and double ones too, than the length and breadth of a pair of indentures? The very conveyances of his lands will scarcely lie in this box, and must th'inheritor himself have no more, ha?

HORATIO. Not a jot more, my lord.

HAMLET. Is not parchment made of sheepskins?

HORATIO. Ay, my lord, and of calveskins too.

HAMLET. They are sheep and calves which seek out assurance in that. I will speak to this fellow. – Whose grave's this, sirrah?

GRAVE-DIGGER. Mine, sir.

(Sings) O a pit of clay for to be made –

HAMLET. I think it be thine indeed, for thou liest in't.

GRAVE-DIGGER. You lie out on't, sir, and therefore 'tis not yours. For my part, I do not lie in't, yet it is mine.

HAMLET. Thou dost lie in't, to be in't and say 'tis thine. 'Tis for the dead, not for the quick: therefore thou liest.

GRAVE-DIGGER. 'Tis a quick lie, sir, 'twill away again from me to you.

HAMLET. What man dost thou dig it for?

GRAVE-DIGGER. For no man, sir.

HAMLET. What woman then?
GRAVE-DIGGER. For none neither.
HAMLET. Who is to be buried in't?
GRAVE-DIGGER. One that was a woman, sir; but rest her soul, she's dead.
HAMLET. How absolute the knave is. We must speak by the card or equivocation will undo us. By the Lord, Horatio, this three years I have took note of it, the age is grown so picked that the toe of the peasant comes so near the heel of the courtier he galls his kibe. – How long hast thou been grave-maker?
GRAVE-DIGGER. Of all the days i'th' year I came to't that day that our last King Hamlet o'ercame Fortinbras.
HAMLET. How long is that since?
GRAVE-DIGGER. Cannot you tell that? Every fool can tell that. It was that very day that young Hamlet was born – he that is mad and sent into England.
HAMLET. Ay, marry. Why was he sent into England?
GRAVE-DIGGER. Why, because a was mad. A shall recover his wits there. Or if a do not, 'tis no great matter there.
HAMLET. Why?
GRAVE-DIGGER. 'Twill not be seen in him there. There the men are as mad as he.
HAMLET. How came he mad?
GRAVE-DIGGER. Very strangely, they say.
HAMLET. How "strangely"?
GRAVE-DIGGER. Faith, e'en with losing his wits.
HAMLET. Upon what ground?
GRAVE-DIGGER. Why, here in Denmark. I have been sexton here, man and boy, thirty years.
HAMLET. How long will a man lie i'th' earth ere he rot?
GRAVE-DIGGER. Faith, if a be not rotten before a die – as we have many pocky corses nowadays that will scarce hold the laying in – a will last you some eight year or nine year. A tanner will last you nine year.
HAMLET. Why he more than another?
GRAVE-DIGGER. Why, sir, his hide is so tanned with his trade that a will keep out water a great while, and your water is a sore decayer of your whoreson dead body. Here's a skull now hath lien you i'th' earth three and twenty years.
HAMLET. Whose was it?
GRAVE-DIGGER. A whoreson mad fellow's it was. Whose do you think it was?
HAMLET. Nay, I know not.

GRAVE-DIGGER. A pestilence on him for a mad rogue! A poured a flagon of Rhenish on my head once. This same skull, sir, was Yorick's skull, the King's jester.

HAMLET. This? *(Takes the skull.)*

GRAVE-DIGGER. E'en that.

HAMLET. Alas, poor Yorick. I knew him, Horatio, a fellow of infinite jest, of most excellent fancy. He hath bore me on his back a thousand times, and now – how abhorred in my imagination it is. My gorge rises at it. Here hung those lips that I have kissed I know not how oft. Where be your gibes now, your gambols, your songs, your flashes of merriment, that were wont to set the table on a roar? Not one now to mock your own grinning? Quite chop-fallen? Now get you to my lady's chamber and tell her, let her paint an inch thick, to this favour she must come. Make her laugh at that. – Prithee, Horatio, tell me one thing.

HORATIO. What's that, my lord?

HAMLET. Dost thou think Alexander looked o' this fashion i'th' earth?

HORATIO. E'en so.

HAMLET. And smelt so? Pah! *(Puts down the skull.)*

HORATIO. E'en so, my lord.

HAMLET. To what base uses we may return, Horatio! Why, may not imagination trace the noble dust of Alexander till a find it stopping a bung-hole?

HORATIO. 'Twere to consider too curiously to consider so.

HAMLET. No, faith, not a jot, but to follow him thither with modesty enough, and likelihood to lead it. Alexander died, Alexander was buried, Alexander returneth to dust, the dust is earth, of earth we make loam, and why of that loam whereto he was converted might they not stop a beer-barrel?
Imperious Caesar, dead and turn'd to clay,
Might stop a hole to keep the wind away.
O that that earth which kept the world in awe
Should patch a wall t'expel the winter's flaw.
But soft, but soft awhile. Here comes the King,
The Queen, the courtiers.

(Enter Bearers with a Coffin, a Priest, King, Queen, Laertes, Lords Attendant.)

Who is this they follow?
And with such maimed rites? This doth betoken
The corse they follow did with desp'rate hand
Fordo it own life. 'Twas of some estate.
Couch we awhile and mark.

LAERTES. What ceremony else?
HAMLET. That is Laertes, a very noble youth. Mark.
LAERTES. What ceremony else?
PRIEST. Her obsequies have been as far enlarg'd
As we have warranty. Her death was doubtful;
And but that great command o'ersways the order,
She should in ground unsanctified been lodg'd
Till the last trumpet: for charitable prayers
Shards, flints, and pebbles should be thrown on her.
Yet here she is allow'd her virgin crants,
Her maiden strewments, and the bringing home
Of bell and burial.
LAERTES. Must there no more be done?
PRIEST. No more be done.
We should profane the service of the dead
To sing sage requiem and such rest to her
As to peace-parted souls.
LAERTES. Lay her i'th' earth,
And from her fair and unpolluted flesh
May violets spring. I tell thee, churlish priest,
A minist'ring angel shall my sister be
When thou liest howling.
HAMLET. What, the fair Ophelia!
QUEEN *(scattering flowers).* Sweets to the sweet. Farewell.
I hop'd thou shouldst have been my Hamlet's wife:
I thought thy bride-bed to have deck'd, sweet maid,
And not have strew'd thy grave.
LAERTES. O, treble woe
Fall ten times treble on that cursed head
Whose wicked deed thy most ingenious sense
Depriv'd thee of. – Hold off the earth awhile,
Till I have caught her once more in mine arms.
(Leaps in the grave.)
Now pile your dust upon the quick and dead,
Till of this flat a mountain you have made
T'o'ertop old Pelion or the skyish head
Of blue Olympus.
HAMLET. What is he whose grief
Bears such an emphasis, whose phrase of sorrow
Conjures the wand'ring stars and makes them stand
Like wonder-wounded hearers? This is I,
Hamlet the Dane.
LAERTES *(grappling with him).*

The devil take thy soul!
HAMLET. Thou pray'st not well.
I prithee take thy ringers from my throat,
For though I am not splenative and rash,
Yet have I in me something dangerous,
Which let thy wiseness fear. Hold off thy hand.
KING. Pluck them asunder.
QUEEN. Hamlet! Hamlet!
ALL. Gentlemen!
HORATIO. Good my lord, be quiet.
HAMLET. Why, I will fight with him upon this theme
Until my eyelids will no longer wag.
QUEEN. O my son, what theme?
HAMLET. I lov'd Ophelia. Forty thousand brothers
Could not with all their quantity of love
Make up my sum. What wilt thou do for her?
KING. O, he is mad, Laertes.
QUEEN. For love of God forbear him.
HAMLET. 'Swounds, show me what thou't do.
Woo't weep, woo't fight, woo't fast, woo't tear thyself,
Woo't drink up eisel, eat a crocodile?
I'll do't. Dost come here to whine,
To outface me with leaping in her grave?
Be buried quick with her, and so will I.
And if thou prate of mountains, let them throw
Millions of acres on us, till our ground,
Singeing his pate against the burning zone,
Make Ossa like a wart. Nay, and thou'lt mouth,
I'll rant as well as thou.
QUEEN. This is mere madness,
And thus awhile the fit will work on him.
Anon, as patient as the female dove
When that her golden couplets are disclos'd,
His silence will sit drooping.
HAMLET. Hear you, sir,
What is the reason that you use me thus?
I lov'd you ever. But it is no matter.
Let Hercules himself do what he may,
The cat will mew, and dog will have his day. *(Exit.)*
KING. I pray thee, good Horatio, wait upon him. *(Exit Horatio.)*
(To Laertes) Strengthen your patience in our last night's speech:
We'll put the matter to the present push. –
Good Gertrude, set some watch over your son.

This grave shall have a living monument.
An hour of quiet shortly shall we see;
Till then in patience our proceeding be. *(Exeunt.)*

SCENE II

Enter Hamlet and Horatio.

HAMLET. So much for this, sir. Now shall you see the other.
You do remember all the circumstance?
HORATIO. Remember it, my lord!
HAMLET. Sir, in my heart there was a kind of fighting
That would not let me sleep. Methought I lay
Worse than the mutines in the bilboes. Rashly –
And prais'd be rashness for it: let us know
Our indiscretion sometime serves us well
When our deep plots do pall; and that should learn us
There's a divinity that shapes our ends,
Rough-hew them how we will –
HORATIO. That is most certain.
HAMLET. Up from my cabin,
My sea-gown scarf'd about me, in the dark
Grop'd I to find out them, had my desire,
Finger'd their packet, and in fine withdrew
To mine own room again, making so bold,
My fears forgetting manners, to unseal
Their grand commission; where I found, Horatio –
Ah, royal knavery! – an exact command,
Larded with many several sorts of reasons
Importing Denmark's health, and England's too,
With ho! such bugs and goblins in my life,
That on the supervise, no leisure bated,
No, not to stay the grinding of the axe,
My head should be struck off.
HORATIO. Is't possible?
HAMLET. Here's the commission, read it at more leisure.
But wilt thou hear now how I did proceed?
HORATIO. I beseech you.
HAMLET. Being thus benetted round with villainies –
Or I could make a prologue to my brains,
They had begun the play – I sat me down,
Devis'd a new commission, wrote it fair –

I once did hold it, as our statists do,
A baseness to write fair, and labour'd much
How to forget that learning, but, sir, now
It did me yeoman's service. Wilt thou know
Th'effect of what I wrote?
HORATIO. Ay, good my lord.
HAMLET. An earnest conjuration from the King,
As England was his faithful tributary,
As love between them like the palm might flourish,
As peace should still her wheaten garland wear
And stand a comma 'tween their amities,
And many such-like "as"es of great charge,
That on the view and knowing of these contents,
Without debatement further more or less,
He should those bearers put to sudden death,
Not shriving-time allow'd.
HORATIO. How was this seal'd?
HAMLET. Why, even in that was heaven ordinant.
I had my father's signet in my purse,
Which was the model of that Danish seal,
Folded the writ up in the form of th'other,
Subscrib'd it, gave't th'impression, plac'd it safely,
The changeling never known. Now the next day
Was our sea-fight, and what to this was sequent
Thou knowest already.
HORATIO. So Guildenstern and Rosencrantz go to't.
HAMLET. Why, man, they did make love to this employment.
They are not near my conscience, their defeat
Does by their own insinuation grow.
'Tis dangerous when the baser nature comes
Between the pass and fell incensed points
Of mighty opposites.
HORATIO. Why, what a king is this!
HAMLET. Does it not, think thee, stand me now upon –
He that hath kill'd my king and whor'd my mother,
Popp'd in between th'election and my hopes,
Thrown out his angle for my proper life
And with such coz'nage – is't not perfect conscience
To quit him with this arm? And is't not to be damn'd
To let this canker of our nature come
In further evil?
HORATIO. It must be shortly known to him from England
What is the issue of the business there.

HAMLET. It will be short. The interim is mine.
And a man's life's no more than to say "one".
But I am very sorry, good Horatio,
That to Laertes I forgot myself;
For by the image of my cause I see
The portraiture of his. I'll court his favours.
But sure the bravery of his grief did put me
Into a tow'ring passion.

HORATIO. Peace, who comes here?

(Enter Osric, a Courtier.)

OSRIC. Your Lordship is right welcome back to Denmark.

HAMLET. I humbly thank you sir. – Dost know this waterfly?

HORATIO. No, my good lord.

HAMLET. Thy state is the more gracious, for 'tis a vice to know him. He hath much land and fertile. Let a beast be lord of beasts and his crib shall stand at the king's mess. 'Tis a chuff, but, as I say, spacious in the possession of dirt.

OSRIC. Sweet lord, if your lordship were at leisure, I should impart a thing to you from his Majesty.

HAMLET. I will receive it, sir, with all diligence of spirit. Your bonnet to his right use: 'tis for the head.

OSRIC. I thank your lordship, it is very hot.

HAMLET. No, believe me, 'tis very cold, the wind is northerly.

OSRIC. It is indifferent cold, my lord, indeed.

HAMLET. But yet methinks it is very sultry and hot for my complexion.

OSRIC. Exceedingly, my lord, it is very sultry – as 'twere – I cannot tell how. My lord, his Majesty bade me signify to you that a has laid a great wager on your head. Sir, this is the matter –

HAMLET *(signing to him to put on his hat)*. I beseech you remember –

OSRIC. Nay, good my lord, for my ease, in good faith. Sir, here is newly come to court Laertes – believe me, an absolute gentleman, full of most excellent differences, of very soft society and great showing. Indeed, to speak feelingly of him, he is the card or calendar of gentry; for you shall find in him the continent of what part a gentleman would see.

HAMLET. Sir, his definement suffers no perdition in you, though I know to divide him inventorially would dozy th'arithmetic of memory, and yet but yaw neither, in respect of his quick sail. But, in the verity of extolment, I take him to be a soul of great article and his infusion of such dearth and rareness as, to make true diction of him, his semblable is his mirror and who else would trace him his umbrage, nothing more.

OSRIC. Your lordship speaks most infallibly of him.

HAMLET. The concernancy, sir? Why do we wrap the gentleman in our more rawer breath?

OSRIC. Sir?

HORATIO. Is't not possible to understand in another tongue? You will to't, sir, really.

HAMLET. What imports the nomination of this gentleman?

OSRIC. Of Laertes?

HORATIO. His purse is empty already, all's golden words are spent.

HAMLET. Of him, sir.

OSRIC. I know you are not ignorant –

HAMLET. I would you did, sir. Yet in faith if you did, it would not much approve me. Well, sir?

OSRIC. You are not ignorant of what excellence Laertes is –

HAMLET. I dare not confess that, lest I should compare with him in excellence; but to know a man well were to know himself.

OSRIC. I mean, sir, for his weapon; but in the imputation laid on him, by them in his meed, he's unfellowed.

HAMLET. What's his weapon?

OSRIC. Rapier and dagger.

HAMLET. That's two of his weapons. But well.

OSRIC. The King, sir, hath wagered with him six Barbary horses, against the which he has impawned, as I take it, six French rapiers and poniards, with their assigns, as girdle, hanger, and so. Three of the carriages, in faith, are very dear to fancy, very responsive to the hilts, most delicate carriages, and of very liberal conceit.

HAMLET. What call you the carriages?

HORATIO. I knew you must be edified by the margin ere you had done.

OSRIC. The carriages, sir, are the hangers.

HAMLET. The phrase would be more german to the matter if we could carry a cannon by our sides – I would it might be hangers till then. But on. Six Barbary horses against six French swords, their assigns, and three liberal-conceited carriages – that's the French bet against the Danish. Why is this – impawned, as you call it?

OSRIC. The King, sir, hath laid, sir, that in a dozen passes between yourself and him he shall not exceed you three hits; he hath laid on twelve for nine. And it would come to immediate trial if your lordship would vouchsafe the answer.

HAMLET. How if I answer no?

OSRIC. I mean, my lord, the opposition of your person in trial.

HAMLET. Sir, I will walk here in the hall. If it please his Majesty, it is the breathing time of day with me. Let the foils be brought, the gentleman willing, and the King hold his purpose, I will win for him and I can; if not, I will gain nothing but my shame and the odd hits.

OSRIC. Shall I deliver you so?

HAMLET. To this effect, sir, after what flourish your nature will.

OSRIC. I commend my duty to your lordship.

HAMLET. Yours. *(Exit Osric.)*
A does well to commend it himself, there are no tongues else for's turn.

HORATIO. This lapwing runs away with the shell on his head.

HAMLET. A did comply with his dug before a sucked it. Thus has he – and many more of the same bevy that I know the drossy age dotes on – only got the tune of the time and, out of an habit of encounter, a kind of yeasty collection, which carries them through and through the most fanned and winnowed opinions; and do but blow them to their trial, the bubbles are out.

(Enter a Lord.)

LORD. My lord, his Majesty commended him to you by young Osric, who brings back to him that you attend him in the hall. He sends to know if your pleasure hold to play with Laertes or that you will take longer time.

HAMLET. I am constant to my purposes, they follow the King's pleasure. If his fitness speaks, mine is ready. Now or whensoever, provided I be so able as now.

LORD. The King and Queen and all are coming down.

HAMLET. In happy time.

LORD. The Queen desires you to use some gentle entertainment to Laertes before you fall to play.

HAMLET. She well instructs me. *(Exit Lord.)*

HORATIO. You will lose, my lord.

HAMLET. I do not think so. Since he went into France, I have been in continual practice. I shall win at the odds. Thou wouldst not think how ill all's here about my heart; but it is no matter.

HORATIO. Nay, good my lord.

HAMLET. It is but foolery, but it is such a kind of gaingiving as would perhaps trouble a woman.

HORATIO. If your mind dislike anything, obey it. I will forestall their repair hither and say you are not fit.

HAMLET. Not a whit. We defy augury. There is special providence in the fall of a sparrow. If it be now, 'tis not to come; if it be not to come, it will be now; if it be not now, yet it will come. The readiness is all. Since no man, of aught he leaves, knows aught, what is't to leave betimes? Let be.

(A table prepared. Trumpets, Drums, and Officers with cushions. Enter King, Queen, Laertes, Osric, and all the State, and Attendants with foils and daggers.)

KING. Come, Hamlet, come, and take this hand from me.
(Puts Laertes's hand into Hamlet's.)

HAMLET. Give me your pardon, sir. I have done you wrong;
But pardon't as you are a gentleman.
This presence knows, and you must needs have heard,
How I am punish'd with a sore distraction.
What I have done
That might your nature, honour, and exception
Roughly awake, I here proclaim was madness.
Was't Hamlet wrong'd Laertes? Never Hamlet.
If Hamlet from himself be ta'en away,
And when he's not himself does wrong Laertes,
Then Hamlet does it not, Hamlet denies it.
Who does it then? His madness. If't be so,
Hamlet is of the faction that is wrong'd;
His madness is poor Hamlet's enemy.
Sir, in this audience,
Let my disclaiming from a purpos'd evil
Free me so far in your most generous thoughts
That I have shot my arrow o'er the house
And hurt my brother.

LAERTES. I am satisfied in nature,
Whose motive in this case should stir me most
To my revenge; but in my terms of honour
I stand aloof, and will no reconcilement
Till by some elder masters of known honour
I have a voice and precedent of peace
To keep my name ungor'd. But till that time
I do receive your offer'd love like love
And will not wrong it.

HAMLET. I embrace it freely,
And will this brothers' wager frankly play. –
Give us the foils.

LAERTES. Come, one for me.

HAMLET. I'll be your foil, Laertes. In mine ignorance
Your skill shall like a star i'th' darkest night
Stick fiery off indeed.

LAERTES. You mock me, sir.
HAMLET. No, by this hand.
KING. Give them the foils, young Osric. Cousin Hamlet,
You know the wager?
HAMLET. Very well, my lord.
Your Grace has laid the odds o'th' weaker side.
KING. I do not fear it. I have seen you both,
But since he is better'd, we have therefore odds.
LAERTES. This is too heavy. Let me see another.
HAMLET. This likes me well. These foils have all a length?
OSRIC. Ay, my good lord. *(They prepare to play.)*
(Enter Servants with flagons of wine.)
KING. Set me the stoups of wine upon that table.
If Hamlet give the first or second hit,
Or quit in answer of the third exchange,
Let all the battlements their ordnance fire:
The King shall drink to Hamlet's better breath,
And in the cup an union shall he throw
Richer than that which four successive kings
In Denmark's crown have worn – give me the cups –
And let the kettle to the trumpet speak,
The trumpet to the cannoneer without,
The cannons to the heavens, the heaven to earth,
"Now the King drinks to Hamlet." Come, begin.
And you, the judges, bear a wary eye.
HAMLET. Come on, sir.
LAERTES. Come, my lord. *(They play.)*
HAMLET. One.
LAERTES. No.
HAMLET. Judgment.
OSRIC. A hit, a very palpable hit.
LAERTES. Well, again.
KING. Stay, give me drink. Hamlet this pearl is thine.
Here's to thy health. *(Drums, trumpets, and shot goes off.)*
Give him the cup.
HAMLET. I'll play this bout first. Set it by awhile.
Come. *(They play again.)*
Another hit. What say you?
LAERTES. I do confess't.
KING. Our son shall win.
QUEEN. He's fat and scant of breath.
Here, Hamlet, take my napkin, rub thy brows.
The Queen carouses to thy fortune, Hamlet.

HAMLET. Good madam.
KING. Gertrude, do not drink.
QUEEN. I will, my lord, I pray you pardon me.
(She drinks and offers the cup to Hamlet.)
KING *(aside).* It is the poison'd cup. It is too late.
HAMLET. I dare not drink yet, madam – by and by.
QUEEN. Come, let me wipe thy face.
LAERTES. My lord, I'll hit him now.
KING. I do not think't.
LAERTES *(aside).* And yet it is almost against my conscience.
HAMLET. Come for the third, Laertes. You do but dally.
I pray you pass with your best violence.
I am afeard you make a wanton of me.
LAERTES. Say you so? Come on. *(They play.)*
OSRIC. Nothing neither way.
LAERTES. Have at you now.
(Laertes wounds Hamlet; then, in scuffling, they change rapiers.)
KING. Part them; they are incensed.
HAMLET. Nay, come again.
(He wounds Laertes. The Queen falls.)
OSRIC. Look to the Queen there, ho!
HORATIO. They bleed on both sides. How is it, my lord?
OSRIC. How is't, Laertes?
LAERTES. Why, as a woodcock to mine own springe, Osric.
I am justly kill'd with mine own treachery.
HAMLET. How does the Queen?
KING. She swoons to see them bleed.
QUEEN. No, no, the drink, the drink! O my dear Hamlet!
The drink, the drink! I am poison'd. *(Dies.)*
HAMLET. O villainy! Ho! Let the door be lock'd.
Treachery! Seek it out. *(Exit Osric.)*
LAERTES. It is here, Hamlet. Hamlet, thou art slain.
No medicine in the world can do thee good;
In thee there is not half an hour's life.
The treacherous instrument is in thy hand,
Unbated and envenom'd. The foul practice
Hath turn'd itself on me. Lo, here I lie,
Never to rise again. Thy mother's poison'd.
I can no more. The King – the King's to blame.
HAMLET. The point envenom'd too! Then, venom, to thy work.
(Wounds the king.)
ALL. Treason! treason!
KING. O yet defend me, friends. I am but hurt.

HAMLET. Here, thou incestuous, murd'rous, damned Dane,
Drink off this potion. Is thy union here?
Follow my mother. *(King dies.)*
LAERTES. He is justly serv'd.
It is a poison temper'd by himself.
Exchange forgiveness with me, noble Hamlet.
Mine and my father's death come not upon thee,
Nor thine on me. *(Dies.)*
HAMLET. Heaven make thee free of it. I follow thee.
I am dead, Horatio. Wretched Queen, adieu.
You that look pale and tremble at this chance,
That are but mutes or audience to this act,
Had I but time – as this fell sergeant, Death,
Is strict in his arrest – O, I could tell you –
But let it be. Horatio, I am dead,
Thou livest. Report me and my cause aright
To the unsatisfied.
HORATIO. Never believe it.
I am more an antique Roman than a Dane.
Here's yet some liquor left.
HAMLET. As th'art a man
Give me the cup. Let go, by Heaven I'll ha't.
O God, Horatio, what a wounded name,
Things standing thus unknown, shall I leave behind me.
If thou didst ever hold me in thy heart,
Absent thee from felicity awhile,
And in this harsh world draw thy breath in pain
To tell my story. *(A march afar off and shot within.)*
What warlike noise is this?
(Enter Osric.)
OSRIC. Young Fortinbras, with conquest come from Poland,
To the ambassadors of England gives
This warlike volley.
HAMLET. O, I die, Horatio.
The potent poison quite o'ercrows my spirit.
I cannot live to hear the news from England,
But I do prophesy th'election lights
On Fortinbras. He has my dying voice.
So tell him, with th'occurrents more and less
Which have solicited – the rest is silence. *(Dies.)*
HORATIO. Now cracks a noble heart. Good night, sweet prince,
And flights of angels sing thee to thy rest. *(March within.)*
Why does the drum come hither?

(Enter Fortinbras, and the English Ambassadors, and Soldiers with drum and colours.)

FORTINBRAS. Where is this sight?
HORATIO. What is it you would see?
If aught of woe or wonder, cease your search.
FORTINBRAS. This quarry cries on havoc. O proud Death,
What feast is toward in thine eternal cell,
That thou so many princes at a shot
So bloodily hast struck?
FIRST AMBASSADOR. The sight is dismal;
And our affairs from England come too late.
The ears are senseless that should give us hearing
To tell him his commandment is fulfill'd,
That Rosencrantz and Guildenstern are dead.
Where should we have our thanks?
HORATIO. Not from his mouth,
Had it th'ability of life to thank you.
He never gave commandment for their death.
But since, so jump upon this bloody question,
You from the Polack wars and you from England
Are here arriv'd, give order that these bodies
High on a stage be placed to the view,
And let me speak to th'yet unknowing world
How these things came about. So shall you hear
Of carnal, bloody, and unnatural acts,
Of accidental judgments, casual slaughters,
Of deaths put on by cunning and forc'd cause,
And, in this upshot, purposes mistook
Fall'n on th'inventors' heads. All this can I
Truly deliver.
FORTINBRAS. Let us haste to hear it,
And call the noblest to the audience.
For me, with sorrow I embrace my fortune.
I have some rights of memory in this kingdom,
Which now to claim my vantage doth invite me.
HORATIO. Of that I shall have also cause to speak,
And from his mouth whose voice will draw on more.
But let this same be presently perform'd
Even while men's minds are wild, lest more mischance
On plots and errors happen.
FORTINBRAS. Let four captains
Bear Hamlet like a soldier to the stage,
For he was likely, had he been put on,

To have prov'd most royal; and for his passage,
The soldier's music and the rite of war
Speak loudly for him.
Take up the bodies. Such a sight as this
Becomes the field, but here shows much amiss.
Go, bid the soldiers shoot.

(Exeunt marching, bearing off the bodies, after which a peal of ordnance is shot off.)

A NOTE ON THE TEXT LAYOUT

The text at hand follows the Second Arden Edition of "Hamlet" by Harold Jenkins, first published in 1982 by Methuen & Co. Ltd. Formatting of stage directions was slightly altered for an enhanced reading experience.

AFTERWORD

The story of Hamlet begins ominously without its title character. Instead, the ghostly figure of his recently deceased father takes centre stage, but does not reveal his secrets until securing an audience with his son. From this point on, Hamlet learns of his father's murder by his uncle, and now King of Denmark, Claudius, forcing the young prince to pursue a course of revenge for which he is ill-prepared.

Hamlet vows to "put on an antic disposition" (p. 27) – to feign madness – in order to complete his vengeful task, leaving both his uncle and mother to worry about the unpredictable nature of his actions. All this takes place against a backdrop of mounting political turmoil and the threat of invading forces from Norway's young prince Fortinbras.

Meanwhile, Ophelia, the daughter of court counsellor Polonius, is asked to discourage Hamlet's affections for her and is later distressed to witness one of his bouts of insanity. Unsure if the reasons for Hamlet's erratic behaviour stem from unrequited love or something else, Claudius enlists Rosencrantz and Guildenstern, two of Hamlet's old school friends, to determine the cause, but without success.

To confirm Claudius' guilt, Hamlet uses a stage performance of *The Murder of Gonzago* (itself based on the real-life murder of Marquese Alfonso Gonzaga by his nephew), with the King fleeing at the murder scene. Subsequently, during a heated conversation with his mother Gertrude, Hamlet stabs blindly at an eavesdropper behind the curtain, believing it to be his uncle. Instead he kills Polonius, sending Ophelia into her own insane delirium and forcing Claudius to despatch Hamlet, along with Rosencrantz and Guildenstern, to England with a royal decree for the prince's execution.

Back in Denmark, Laertes is enraged by his father's death and grows madder still following Ophelia's grief-stricken suicide. Offstage, Hamlet learns of Claudius' plan, sends Rosencrantz and Guildenstern to their deaths instead, and returns to Denmark after bargaining with pirates. He is quickly challenged to a fencing duel by Laertes – part of a new plan by the King to kill his nephew via either a poisoned foil or toxic celebratory drink.

During the contest, both Laertes and Hamlet are wounded by the poisoned blade and Gertrude unwittingly drinks from the contaminated chalice. Now aware of his impending fate, Hamlet kills Claudius, before perishing himself, leaving the stage littered with the dead.

The source for much of the action in Hamlet is "Gesta Danorum," written by 12th century Danish theologian Saxo Grammaticus. The text is made up of sixteen books containing a mixture of Norse mythology and medieval history and has proven an invaluable source of information for historians. Shakespeare too found the text useful, with many elements providing inspiration for Hamlet: the murder of the king by a treacherous brother, the swift marriage of the queen to the killer and the falsified insanity of the king's vengeful son Amleth. However, it is unlikely that

Shakespeare had first-hand experience with this text, instead likely relying on a more contemporary version such as that included in Belleforest's translation of the "Histoires Tragiques," published in the late 16th century. However, the most immediate source for Shakespeare's Hamlet is likely to be a now lost play, possibly written by dramatist Thomas Kyd and in performance from 1589. Dubbed "Ur-Hamlet," the play appears to have been based on the tragedies of Roman playwright Seneca and featured a strong revenge theme. The role of the ghost, inciting the protagonist to take action against his murderer, is introduced and would also feature in another play of more certain origin, Kyd's "The Spanish Tragedy." Kyd's work was seemingly popular and influential in the Elizabethan theatre scene and with its use of a play-within-a-play and vengeful ghost, it is easy to see why Kyd has been claimed as the author of Ur-Hamlet and an inspiration for Shakespeare's own text.

Although there are evidently versions of the story, extant or lost, that pre-date Shakespeare's, it is his text that continues to endure.

However, despite being a near constant presence on the English stage, in many ways Hamlet remains an elusive play, particularly where its origins are concernet. Believed to have been written sometime between 1599 and 1602, the first concrete evidence of the play's existence comes in July 1602, when Hamlet is recorded in the Register of the Stationers' Company, indicating that the play had been recently performed by the Lord Chamberlain's Men.

The earliest surviving written edition of the play, however, is the First Quarto published in 1603 under the name „The Tragicall Historie of Hamlet, Prince of Denmarke." Unknown to modern scholars until 1823, this so-called Bad Quarto is significantly shorter than most commonly performed versions of Hamlet and has been labelled as a pirated or inauthentic text. Despite these criticisms, the First Quarto does offer valuable insights into the common practices of Elizabethan theatre by way of its extensive stage directions.

The Second Quarto edition, published in 1604–1605, is nearly double the length of the earlier text but still contains a number of printing errors. By contrast, the first release of Shakespeare's complete works in 1623, the First Folio, contains a version of Hamlet that adds some important passages missing from the Second Quarto, but omits others. Modern interpretations of the text, therefore, are usually comprised of a mixture of the Second Quarto and First Folio editions. Every editor and director since the play's creation has had to wrestle with the decision of which lines represent the true essence of the play and which do not.

Even taking into account the richness of vocabulary found in other examples of Elizabethan theatre, Shakespeare's Hamlet is a startlingly complex work. It is not only the author's longest play, it is arguably his most difficult, with directors, critics and audiences having argued for centuries over the key character's motives and the text's philosophical and psychoanalytic implications. At nearly 4,000 lines long, Hamlet cannot only prove challenging for audiences, but also its performers. The lead actor must memorise and deliver nearly 40 per cent of the play's lines, including a number of meandering and intricate soliloquies. Actors will also have the honour, and burden, of performing some of the most famous speeches in the English language, including the oft-quoted "To be, or not to be."

Evidence suggests that Hamlet was one of Shakespeare's most popular plays during his lifetime, with only Henry VI Part 1, Richard III and Pericles proving more highly sought after by audiences. In fact, Hamlet carries the honour of being the first Shakespearian play to be performed outside of Europe. The crew of the Red Dragon ship performed the tragedy off the coast of Sierra Leone in 1607 and the play would find its way to Indonesia just two years later. It was not uncommon for travelling merchants and sailors to conduct performances as a means of entertainment, but the far-flung enactments still stand as testament to Hamlet's early popularity.

Despite the play's medieval setting, these earliest productions would have seen performers in contemporary Elizabethan dress. In the years since, however, many directors have used artistic license to transport the play to various locations and time periods. Different aspects of the text have been emphasised or repressed in order to better understand, or pass comment on, the social, cultural or political context during the time of performance – essentially, to hold a "mirror up to nature" (p. 51).

Like many of Shakespeare's other famous works: Romeo and Juliet, Macbeth and King Lear included, the story of Hamlet existed long before the "Bard of Avon" first put pen to paper. Shakespeare's genius, therefore, does not lie in the invention of characters, settings or even the plots of his plays. Rather, it is the lyrical poeticism, imbued within the very fabric of his work that elevates his telling far above that of those who have come before or after him. Shakespeare's Hamlet has a universal quality that permits it to tell us much more than the story of a Danish prince spurred on to avenge his father. Anger, doubt, despair, remorse and love – these eternally human qualities at the heart of the play – ensure that it remains just as relevant today as it was to those early Elizabethan audiences.

TIMELINE

1564	William Shakespeare is born to John Shakespeare, an alderman and prestigious glover and wool dealer, and Mary Arden, daughter of a wealthy, landowning farmer. He is baptized on 26 April in Stratford-upon-Avon, his actual birthday is unknown.
1571–1578	William Shakespeare presumably visits the King's New School in Stratford, where he is supposed to have been taught in Latin, ancient Greek, history, ethics and poetry.
1582	William Shakespeare marries 8 year older Anne Hathaway, daughter to a farmer.
1582–1592	Thomas Kyd writes The Spanish Tragedy. Featuring the character of a ghost and a theme centring on revenge, the play is believed to have been a major influence on Shakespeare when writing Hamlet.
1583	William Shakespeare and his wife have their first daughter, Susanna, born only six months after their marriage.
1585	Their twins, Hamnet and Judith, are born.
1585–1592	William Shakespeare's so-called lost years, as little is known about his life during that time. He is believed to have left his family and moved to London, where he worked as a playwright and performer.
1589	Earliest references to a version of the Hamlet story by an unknown author, dubbed "Ur-Hamlet." Despite seemingly being well-known at the time, the play was not published and is now lost. Possible authors include Kyd and Shakespeare himself.
1589–1590	William Shakespeare is believed to have written his first play, Henry VI, Part One.
1592	William Shakespeare is first mentioned as part of London's theatre scene. Robert Greene calls him in Groatworth of Wit an "upstart crow" and attacks him for borrowing ideas from other plays for his own.
1592–1594	London's theatres are shut down due to the plague.
1594	William Shakespeare joins the Lord Chamberlain's Men, a theatre group that also includes well-known actor Richard Burbage and comic Will Kemp.
1594–1596	William Shakespeare writes A Midsummer Night's Dream, Richard II and the greatest love story of all time, Romeo & Juliet.
1596	William Shakespeare's son, Hamnet, dies at the age of 11, presumably from the bubonic plague.
1600	William Shakespeare is believed to have written one of his greatest plays, Hamlet.

1603	(mid) – April 1604, London's theatres are shut down due to the plague.
1603	The First Quarto version of Hamlet is published. The so-called Bad Quarto, it contains many textual inconsistencies and the names of prominent characters are changed.
1604	The Second Quarto is printed and is significantly longer than the first. However, it still omits many lines present in modern versions.
1605	William Shakespeare is believed to have written All's Well That Ends Well and King Lear.
1606	William Shakespeare is believed to have written Macbeth and Antony and Cleopatra.
1608–1610	London's theatres are shut down due to the plague from spring 1608 until early 1610.
1616	William Shakespeare dies on 23 April, and is buried in Holy Trinity Church in Stratford-upon-Avon two days later.
1623	John Hemminges and Henry Condell, two of William Shakespeare's fellow actors from the King's Men, publish 36 of his 37 plays in a collection known as the First Folio. Due to the many differences found between the various versions of Hamlet, modern editions often combine elements of both the Second Quarto and the First Folio.

GLOSSARY

DRAMATIS PERSONAE

foppish – being overly concerned with appearance and mannerisms
courtier – someone who regularly attends the royal court
Elsinore – A city in east Denmark and the setting for the play

ACT I, SCENE I

2 to unfold s.o. – to reveal/ identify s.o.
14 rival – partner, colleague
15 ho – hey
16 liegeman – subjects or servants of
16 Dane – the Danish Kings
17 Give you good night – God give you goodnight. Sleep well.
18 to relieve s.o. – to release someone from duty
26 fantasy – imagination
28 touching – regarding or concerning
28 seen of us – seen by us
29 to entreat – to ask seriously
32 to approve – to prove, to confirm them to be truthful
33 tush – an exclamation of impatience and disbelief
34 to assail – to attack or (in this case) to convince
35 fortified – defended
38 last night of all – only last night
39 yond – yonder, used to refer to something in the distance
39 pole – northern pole star, called the North Star
40 t'illume – to illuminate, to brighten
43 peace – quiet
43 break thee off – stop speaking
46 a – he
46 to mark sth. – to observe or look upon sth.
47 to harrow – to disturb, to scare
48 It would be spoke to – It wants to be spoken to. It was believed that ghosts could not speak before being spoken to.
49 to usurp sth. – to take without permission
51 the majesty of buried Denmark – the noble form of the deceased Danish King
52 sometimes – formerly
53 to stalk – to walk slowly
58 on't – of it
60 sensible – relating to the senses
60 avouch – assertion or confirmation
64 th'ambitious Norway – the King of Norway
64 to combat s.o. – to battle, to fight s.o.
65 parle – negotiation or exchange of words
66 to smite – to strike firmly
66 sledded – riding in sledges
66 Polack – Polish
68 jump – just
69 martial – military
71 in the gross and scope – in the general drift
72 eruption – violent disturbance
73 good now – very well
75 to toil – to cause toil, to wear out
75 subject – subjects
76 cast – manufacture from molten metal
76 brazen – made of brass

77 mart – trading
78 impress – to force into service, conscription
78 shipwright – shipbuilder
78 sore – difficult, tiresome
80 to be toward – to be about to happen
83 whisper – rumour
84 even but now – even just now
86 to prick s.o. on – to goad or spur someone to do something
86 emulate – competitive
87 to dare s.o. – to challenge s.o.
87 Hamlet – the deceased King Hamlet
88 to esteem – to think of
89 sealed compact – legally binding contract
90 to ratify – to make valid or official
90 heraldry – the system of royal protocol or rank
92 to be seized of sth. – to gain legal possession of
93 moiety – portion
93 competent – sufficient, adequate
94 to gage – to pledge
94f which had return'd / To the inheritance of Fortinbras – which would have been part of Fortinbras' inheritance
96 cov'nant – contract
97 carriage – carrying out
97 article – specified clause in the contract
99 unimproved – untested and without discipline
99 mettle – spirit or temperament
100 skirts – outskirts, the outlying areas
101 to shark up – to greedily gather up
101 list – gang, troop
101 resolute – lawless people
103 stomach – appetite
105 of – from
106 compulsatory – compulsory
109 head – cause
110 post-haste – great speed
110 rummage – turmoil, strife
112 to sort – to agree with the present situation
112 portentous – ominous
114 question – cause
115 mote – particle of dust
116 palmy – mighty. The palm was a symbol of victory in Rome.
117 ere – before
117 Julius – Julius Caesar (100 BC–44 BC), Roman statesman, general and author
118 tenantless – empty
118 sheeted – covered with a burial shroud
119 to squeak – to squeal, to speak in anguish
119 to gibber – to talk nonsense
120 train – trail
121 disasters – dark spots on the sun's surface
121 the moist star – the moon
122 Neptune – god of freshwater and the sea in Roman mythology
123 almost to doomsday – almost to death
124 precurse – precusor
125 harbinger – omen
128 climature – climate
129 soft – stop
130 to cross s.o. – to walk across s.o.
130 to blast – to destroy
136 privy – aware of, to have knowlege of
137 happily – perhaps
139 to uphoard – to be hoarded up, collected
140 to extort – to wrongfully acquire
143 partisan – a long-handled axe

152 crew – crowed
153 to start – to act startled
155 morn – morning
156 lofty – high-sounding
157 the god of day – the sun
159 extravagant – without restraint
159 erring – wandering
159 to hie – to hurry
160 confine – his place of confinement
161 object – the previous moment
161 probation – proof
163 'gainst – before, in anticipation of
164 Saviour – Jesus Christ
167 wholesome – healthy
167 to strike – referencing the belief that planets and stars had evil influence
168 to take – to enchant with a spell
169 hallow'd – holy
169 gracious – touched by heavenly grace
171 russet – a reddy-brown colour
171 clad – clothed
174 to impart – to make known
178 as needful in our loves, fitting our duty – as required by our love for and duty towards him

ACT I, SCENE II
182 green – fresh
182 that it us befitted – that it was fitting, proper
184 to contract – to contain
185 discretion – judgement, reason
188 sometime – former
188 sister – sister-in-law, his brother's wife
189 jointress – widow with rights to property formerly owned by her husband
190 as 'twere – as it were, in the past
191 dropping – cast downwards in grief
192 dirge – a mounful song, often associated with a funeral
193 dole – sorrow
194 to bar sth. – to ignore or exclude sth.
195f to go along with sth. – to support sth.
198 supposal – estimate
199 by – because of
200 disjoint – disjointed, incoherent
200 out of frame – out of sorts, dislocated
201 colleagued – joined
203 to import – to regard, to concern
207 writ – written
209 impotent – frail, powerless
209 bedrid – bedridden, confined to bed
211 gait – progress, proceeding
211 levy – raised troops
212 proportion – quota, group
218 dilated – detailed
221 nothing – not at all
223 suit – request
225 to lose one's voice – to waste one's words
227 native – connected, closely related
228 instrumental – connected
230 dread – deeply revered
231 leave – permission
239 laboursome – tiresome, wearying
239 petition – request
239f at last / Upon his will I seal'd my hard consent – finally I gave my consent
241 to beseech – to ask, to beg
242 take thy fair hour – take your leave
243 graces – virtues

244 cousin – general term for relative
245 kin – family member. By marrying Hamlet's mother, the King is more closely related to Hamlet.
245 kind – affectionate. Hamlet is angry that Claudius has married his mother.
248 nighted – dark, as of the night
250 to vail – to cover
252 common – frequent, but Hamlet uses the term to mean vulgar or crass.
257 inky – dark in colour, like ink
259 windy – flighty, insincere
259 suspiration – sigh
260 fruitful – producing a lot
261 haviour – behaviour
261 visage – face
262 shape – outward expression
263 to denote – to depict, to show
265 to pass sth. – to exceed, to surpass
266 trappings – ornaments
270f to be bound to do sth. – to be compelled to do sth.
271 filial – relating to a son or daughter
271 term – period of time
272 obsequious – relating to funeral rites
272 to persever – to persevere, to continue
273 condolement – sorrow, mourning
274 impious – lacking respect for God's will
275 incorrect – disobedient
276 unfortified – weak, without the fortification of religion
277 unschool'd – uneducated
280 peevish – childishly stubborn
281 fie – used to express disgust
285 corse – corpse
287 unprevailing – unavailing, pointless
293 school – university
294 retrograde – opposed to, against
296 eye – looks, watch
298 to lose one's prayers – to have one's prayers go unanswered
300 in all my best – to the best of my ability
301 why – well
304 grace – honour
305 jocund health – joyous toast
307 rouse – drinking session
307 to bruit – to celebrate, to echo
309 too too – repeated for emphasis
309 sullied – dirtied, made impure
310 to resolve o.s. – to dissolve
311 the Everlasting – God
312 canon – law, decree
312 self-slaughter – suicide
314 uses – habits, ways of doing things
317 merely – entirely, completely
320 Hyperion – one of the titans in Greek mythology and the father of Helios, the god of the sun
320 satyr – one of the male companions of Dionysus, the god of wine, with horse-like features in Greek mythology
321 to beteem – to allow
327 or ere – or before
329 Niobe – figure in Greek mythology whose offspring were killed. She is reported to have continued crying even after being turned into a stone.
330 to want – to lack

330 discourse of reason – ability to reason

333 Hercules – Greek demi-god and son of Zeus, known for his immense strength. Featured on the emblem of the globe theatre to which the Shakespeare group belonged

334 unrighteous – insincere

335 flushing – redness

335 galled – sore

336 to post – to hurry

337 dexterity – clever nimbleness

337 incestuous – forbidden relationship, because as she is his brother's wife, Gertrude and Claudius are related

343 change – exchange

347 good even – good evening

349 truant disposition – idle, lazy nature

352 truster – authoriser

352f report / Against yourself – report that discredits yourself

359 hard – closely

360 thrift – Hamlet blames the swiftness of marriage on purely economic reasons.

360 bak'd meat – food laid out for the funeral

362 would I had met – I would rather have met

362 dear – greatest

362 foe – enemy

372 to season – to control

372 admiration – wonder

373 attent – attentive

373 to deliver – to reveal

380 at point – in every detail

380 cap-à-pie – from head to foot

382 stately – formal

383 oppress'd – stunned (by fear)

384 to distil – to dissolve

385 act – influence

387 dreadful – full of terror and dread

389f both in time / Form of the thing – both the time and shape described were correct.

396f to address o.s. to sth. – prepare to speak

398 even then – at that moment

409 beaver – helmet visor

411 countenance – face

417 to tell – to count

420 grizzled – grey

422 sable – black

423 perchance – perhaps

423 to warrant – to assure

424 person – form, likeness

425 to gape – to open

426 to hold one's peace – to be quiet, to not say anything

428 tenable – possible to be held

429 whatsomever – whatever

429 to hap – to happen

431 to requite – to reward

436 to doubt – to suspect

ACT I, SCENE III

439 necessaries – his belongings, luggage

439 to embark – to be ready to leave

440 as – whenever

440 to give benefit – to allow

441 convoy is assistant – transport of letters is possible

443 trifling – admiration

444 to hold – to consider

444 fashion – passing fancy

444 toy – childish impulse

445 violet – a type of flower

445 primy – early

446 forward – impulsive

447 suppliance – fulfilment

448 but so – than that

449 crescent – growing

450 thews – physical size, muscles

450 this temple – body

450 to wax – to grow
452 withal – with it
453 soil – stain
453 cautel – trickery
453 to besmirch – to tarnish
455 his greatness weigh'd – his greatness considered
457 unvalu'd – ordinary, not royal
458 to carve for o.s. – to choose for o.s.
460 to circumscribe – to restrict
461 yielding – consent
461 body – body politic, i.e. the state of Denmark
466 main – general
466 withal – along with it
468 credent – trusting
468 list – listen to
469 chaste treasure – virginity
470 unmaster'd – unrestrained, lacking control
470 importunity – persistence
472 rear – to the back of one's mind
474 chary – cautious, modest
474 prodigal – reckless
476 to scape – to escape
476 calumnious – slanderous
477 canker – canker-worm, one that destroys plants
477 to gall – to wound
478 button – bud
478 to disclose – to open
480 blastment – injury, blight
482 to itself rebels – rebels against itself
485 ungracious – ungodly
487 puff'd – bloated with pride
487 libertine – indulgent person
488 primrose – a flowering plant
488 dalliance – casual sexual relationship
489 to reck – to heed
489 rede – advice
489 to fear s.o. – to worry about s.o.
495 to be stayed for – to be waited for
496 precept – rule
498 unproportion'd – unruly
499 familiar – friendly
499 vulgar – tasteless, lacking sophistication
500 their adoption tried – their worthiness tested
501 to grapple – to hold
502 to dull – to blunt, to soften
502 entertainment – i.e. shaking hands
503 unfledg'd – untested
505 opposed – opponent
507 censure – opinion
508 costly – expensive
508 habit – clothes
509 fancy – elaborate
509 gaudy – extravagant
511 they in France of the best rank and station – have the most distinguished clothes
515 husbandry – economy
519 to season – to make more durable
521 to tend – to await
528 marry – short for "by the Virgin Mary", used instead of "indeed"
528 to bethink – to think of
529 of late – lately, recently
531 bounteous – generous
532 to put sth. on s.o. – to convey to s.o.
535 to behove – to befit
536 to give up – to reveal
537 tenders – offers
539 green – inexperienced, naive
540 unsifted – untested
540 perilous – dangerous
544 ta'en – taken
545 sterling – currency
545 to tender – to value
546 to crack the wind – to wear out
547 to run sth. – to ride (in this case a horse)

548 to importune – to plead persistently
550 go to – dismissive remark
551 countenance – authority
553 springe – traps
553 woodcock – a bird that is easily caught, considered gullible
554 prodigal – prodigally, generously
556 extinct – extinguishing
559 scant – reserved, modest
560 your entreatments – negotiations, discussions
561 to parley – to negotiate, usually issued as a request from the enemy
563 tether – rope used to restrict movement
564 in few – in short
565 broker – a go-between or pimp
566 dye – colour
566 investments – clothes
567 implorator – pleaders
567 suit – request
568 sanctified – holy
568 bawds – a woman in charge of a brothel, again suggesting a pimp
569 this is for all – in summary
573 come your ways – come along

ACT I, SCENE IV

575 shrewdly – sharply
576 nipping – cold
576 eager – biting
580 held his wont – is accustomed to, usually
b581 ordnance – cannon
582 rouse – drinking party
583 wassail – revelry
583 and the swagg'ring upspring reels – drunkenly performing a German dance
584 to drain – to drink
584 Rhenish – Rhenish wine, from the area around the Rhine
585 kettle-drum – type of drum
585 to bray out – to blare out
586 pledge – promise
590 breach – breaking
591f This heavy-headed revel … / … of other nations – other countries criticise Denmark for its revelry
593 to clepe – to call
594 addition – accomplishments
596 pith – essence, core
596 marrow – centre, core
596 attribute – courage
598 mole – natural blemish
601 o'ergrowth – overgrowth
602 pale – limit
602 fort – fortress
603 to overleaven – to overcome, to be excessive
604 plausive – worthy of applause
605 stamp – mark
606 livery – uniform
606 Fortune's star – caused by the evil influence of the stars
608 to undergo – to have
609 to take corruption – to become corrupted
610 dram – small drink
611 to dout – to doubt
613 minister – God's ministers, angels
614 health – benevolence
614 goblin – demon
615 blast – destruction
617 questionable – that encourages questions
621 canoniz'd – consecrated, buried in church
621 hearsed – entombed
622 cerements – cloth used to wrap a corpse
622 sepulchre – tomb
623 inurn'd – buried
624 to ope – to open
624 ponderous – heavy

625 to cast up – to expel, to force out
628 hideous – horrifying
629 disposition – temperament, composure
630 reaches – grasp, understanding
633 impartment – communication
635 to wave – to invite, to beckon
635 removed – distant
639 fee – worth
645 to beetle – to overhang
647 sovereignty – control
651 fathom – measurement used to refer to water depth
655 to be ruled – to be controlled
656 petty – insignificant
656 artire – artery
657 Nemean lion – vicious creature in Greek mythology, slain by Hercules
657 nerve – tendon, sinew
658 to unhand – to let go
661 to wax – to grow
663 to have after – to follow
663 issue – outcome

ACT I, SCENE V

667 to mark s.o. – to listen to s.o.
668 sulph'rous – relating to sulphur, which was associated with Hell
676 to fast – to go without food
677 in my days of nature – when he was alive
678 to purge – to cleanse
678 but – if it were not
683 knotted and combined – interlocked, styled
683 lock – hair
684 an end – on end
685 quill – pointy spine
685 fretful – anxious, distressed
685 porpentine – porcupine
686 this eternal blazon – this proclamation of the eternal world, i.e. afterlife
690 unnatural – a crime against nature
692 in the best – even at best
695 meditation – thought
696 to sweep – to act suddenly
696 apt – ready
697 dull – sluggish
698 Lethe – one of the five rivers of the Greek underworld, drinking from which caused complete forgetfulness
698 wharf – bank
700 to give out – to say or suggest
702 forged – faked
702 process – report
703 rankly – excessively
706 prophetic – able to predict the future
707 adulterate – adulterous
713 dignity – worth
715f to decline upon s.o. – to fall for someone so worthless, i.e. Claudius
716 wretch – despicable person
718 but virtue, as it never will be mov'd – but as true virtue cannot be destroyed
719 lewdness – crudeness, vulgarity
721 to sate o.s. – to satisfy o.s.
721 celestial – heavenly
722 to prey on sth. – to desire sth.
722 garbage – filth
726 secure – carefree
727 hebenon – poisonous substance
727 vial – small container
728 porch – entrance
729 leperous – producing skin disfigurement similar to leprosy
729 distilment – liquid
732 alley – narrow passageway
733f to posset / to curd – to thicken, to clot

734 eager – acidic
736 tetter – eruption of the skin
736 to bark about – to be covered in a bark-like crust
737 lazar-like – like Lazarus, who had leprosy
740 at once – instantly
740 to dispatch s.o. – to kill s.o.
742 unhousel'd – without having received Holy Communion
742 disappointed – unprepared
742 unanel'd – without being anointed with holy oil
743 reck'ning – confession
743 account – judgement
748 luxury – lust
749 howsomever – however
749 pursuest – pursues
750 to taint – to pollute, to stain
751 aught – anything
754 matin – morning
755 gins – begins
755 uneffectual – ineffective
757 host – angels
758 to couple – to add
759 instant – instantly
760 to bear s.o. up – to hold s.o. up
762 distracted – distressed
763 table – journal
764 fond – foolish
765 saw – saying
765 form – images
765 pressure – impressions
767 commandment – command
770 pernicious – wicked
772 tables – journals
772 meet – appropriate
772 to set sth. down – to write sth. down
775 word – phrase
780 to secure – to protect
782 hillo – hello
786 wonderful – astonishing
791 once – ever
795 but he's – who is not
795 arrant – notorious
798 circumstance – detail, talk
804 whirling – extravagant
809 honest – genuine
810 between us – the secret between Hamlet and the ghost
811 to overmaster – to repress
811 as you may – if you want
823 truepenny – honest person
824 cellarage – cellars
829 hic et ubique – Latin for "here and everywhere"
836 pioner – pioneer, soldier responsible for digging trenches
836 to remove – to move
845 antic – bizarre, erratic
847 encumber'd – folded
848 doubtful – ambiguous
849 and if we would – if we would
850 to list – to wish
850 There be and if they might – There are those that might explain this, if they could
851 giving out – revelation, suggestion
855 perturbed – unsettled
858 friending – friendship
859 God willing – if it pleases God
861 time – age, general state of things
861 out of joint – disjointed, disturbed

ACT II, SCENE I

864 note – piece of advice
866 marvellous – marvellously
870 inquire me first – inquire for me first
870 Dansker – Danes
871 and how – and how they are living
871 means – income
871 to keep – to live
873 encompassment – roundabout way of questioning
873 drift – aim

876 to take – to pretend
882 to put sth. on s.o. – to say to s.o.
883 forgery – lie
885 wanton – boisterous, immodest
885 slip – flaw
889 drabbing – using prostitutes
891 to season – to modify, to give reasons for
893 to be open to sth. – to be held accountable for sth.
893 incontinency – excessive sexual promiscuity
894 quaintly – lightly, delicately
895 taint – fault
897 savageness – wildness
897 unreclaimed – untamed
898 of general assault – of which all are susceptible
901 drift – plan
902 fetch – well-thought out
902 of warrant – strategy
903 sully – blemish
904 as 'twere – as if he were
904 a little soil'd i'th' working – slightly tarnished by life
906 party in converse – the person you are speaking to
906 to sound s.o. – to question s.o.
907 having ever – if he has ever
907 prenominate – previously mentioned
909 to close with s.o. – to agree with s.o.
909 in this consequence – in what is about to follow
911 addition – way of addressing
914 by the mass – by the Eucharist, an expression of annoyance with o.s.
915 to leave – to finish
921 o'ertook in's rouse – overcome by his drunkeness
922 to fall out – to disagree with
922 tennis – sport considered particularly popular in France
924 videlicet – Latin for "that is to say"
924 brothel – place to visit prostitutes
926 carp – type of fish
927 reach – perception
928 windlass – roundabout method
928 assay of bias – indirect attempt
930 lecture – lesson
931 to have s.o. – to understand s.o.
932 God buy ye – God be with you
935 to ply – to pursue
938 to affright – to frighten
940 closet – chamber, room
941 doublet – close fitting jacket
941 unbrac'd – undone
942 foul'd – stained with dirt
943 ungarter'd – untied, falling down
943 down-gyved to his ankle – fallen down
945 piteous – miserable
945 purport – expression
946 to loose – to set free
953 perusal – studying
954 as – as if
958 bulk – body
962 o' – of
963 to the last – until the last moment
965 ecstasy – frenzy, madness
966 property – nature
966 to fordo – to destroy
972 to repel – to reject
975 to quote – to observe
975 to trifle – to toy
976 to wrack – to wreck, to dishonour
976 beshrew – curse
976 jealousy – suspicion
977 our age – as an old man
978 to cast beyond o.s. in sth. –

to overreach with one's opinions
981f which, being kept close, might move / More grief to hide than hate to utter love – which may cause more unhappiness by being hid than if it was revealed

ACT II, SCENE II
985 moreover that – in addition to the fact that
989 sith – since
995 neighbour'd – close to, familiar with
996 vouchsafe your rest – allowed to rest here
999 to glean – to obtain
1001 to open – to reveal, to make known
1004 to adhere to s.o. – to be attached to s.o.
1005 gentry – coutesy
1006 to expend – to spend, to use up
1007 supply – fulfilment
1008 visitation – visit
1010 sovereign – royal
1010 of – over
1011 pleasure – desire
1013 in the full bent – to the full extent
1021 practice – action
1026 liege – superior, often royal
1030 policy – political scheming
1035 fruit – dessert
1036 to do grace to s.o. – to honour s.o.
1038 distemper – mental derangement, illness
1039 main – the chief matter
1040 o'er-hasty – over-hasty, too quick
1041 to sift – to question
1041 him – in this case, Polonius
1042 brother – used merely as a token of goodwill
1044 upon our first – when we first raised the matter
1047 better look'd into – when inspected more closely
1049 impotence – weakness
1050 arrest – order to cease military activity
1052 in fine – in conclusion
1054 to give th'assay of arms against s.o. – to take up military action against s.o.
1056 fee – payment
1058 to levy – to impose
1059 entreaty – request
1062 regard – conditions
1062 allowance – permission
1063 it likes us well – Claudius is pleased and uses the royal "us"
1064 at our more consider'd time – at a more appropriate time
1066 well-took – well carried out
1069 to expostulate – to discuss
1078 matter – detail
1078 art – unnecessary flamboyance
1086 effect defective – defective trait
1088 to perpend – to consider
1091 to surmise – to conclude
1092 beautified – beautiful
1094 these – these phrases in the letter
1097 faithful – truthful to the letter's content
1102 numbers – verse
1102f to reckon – to number metrically, to fit them into his poetry
1105 machine – body
1105 is to him – belongs to him, is living
1108 more above – moreover
1108 soliciting – offering
1109 to fall out – to occur
1114 fain – gladly
1115 on the wing – borne by a strong wing

1119 table-book – capable of containing secrets, but not acting on them

1120 or given my heart a winking mute and dumb – or closed the eyes of my heart

1121 with idle sight – without considering its significance

1122 round – roundly, thoroughly

1123 mistress – daughter

1123 to bespeak s.o. – to address s.o.

1124 out of thy star – beyond your reach or status

1125 prescript – instruction

1126 to lock o.s. from s.o.'s resort – to shut o.s. away from s.o.'s visits

1131 watch – sleepless state

1132 lightness – light-headedness

1132 declension – decline

1133 to rave – to talk incoherently as if mad

1140 circumstance – evidence

1142 centre – centre of the earth

1142 to try – to test

1143 four hours together – used to indicate an unspecified, but long period of time

1146 arras – a hanging tapestry

1148 thereon – as a result of

1150 carter – cart drivers

1153 to board – to attack with speech

1153 give me leave – leave me to be alone

1155 God-a-mercy – God have mercy, a way of saying thanks

1157 excellent – throroughly

1157 fishmonger – one who sells fish

1164f a good kissing carrion – a piece of rotting flesh kissed by the sun

1167 conception – double-meaning suggesting understanding and also becoming pregnant

1168 to conceive – to become pregnant

1169 How say you by that? – What do you mean by that?

1169f to harp on sth. – to dwell on sth.

1171 extremity – extreme emotions

1175 matter – content

1178 rogue – a dishonest individual

1180 to purge – to exude

1180 amber – a thick resin produced by trees

1181 hams – legs

1183 honesty – gentlemanly

1184 old as – as old as

1188f pregnant – full of meaning

1189 happiness – fortuitousness

1191 to deliver – this continues the terminology of child-birth

1191 suddenly – immediately

1205 indifferent – average, ordinary

1207 Fortune – Fortuna, Roman goddess of fortune, personification of luck

1207 the very button – the very top

1212 privates – ordinary citizens, but also suggesting genitals

1214 strumpet – prostitute

1218 at the hands of – caused by

1224 ward – prison cell

1230 bounded – bound, contained

1236 airy – flimsy, weak

1238 body – only unambitious beggars have bodies of substance, if ambition is but a shadow

1239 outstretched – reaching ambitiously

1240 fay – faith

1240 to reason – to think straight

1241 to wait upon s.o. – to accompany s.o.
1242 to sort – to include
1244 to attend s.o. – to serve
1244 beaten – well-trodden, long-established
1249 inclining – inclination, Hamlet asks if they came of their own accord
1250 justly – truthfully
1252 but to th' purpose – a double-meaning where Hamlet asks them to be brief or recognises that they are not telling the truth
1253f modesty – honesty
1254 craft – skill
1254 to colour – to conceal, to hide
1257 to conjure – to ask
1258 consonancy – friendship
1260 proposer – questioner
1260 to charge s.o. with sth. – to ask someone urgently
1260 even – fair
1263f to hold off – to withhold something
1266 anticipation – revelation
1267 discovery – Hamlet speaks first so that he "discovers" Rosencrantz and Guildenstern's reasons rather than them having to reveal them.
1267 to moult – to shed feathers
1269 all custom of exercises – all his usual habits
1270 heavily – sadly, despondently
1270 disposition – mood
1271 promontory – a piece of land jutting out into the sea
1271 canopy – a covering held above something
1272 brave – splendid
1273 to fret – to adorn, to cover
1274 pestilent – destructive
1274 congregation – group
1274f What piece of work – what a wonderful creation
1276 express – exact
1277 apprehension – understanding
1278 paragon – perfect example
1286 Lenten entertainment – poor reception, appropriate for Lent
1287 to cote – to overtake
1291 foil – sword
1291 target – shield
1291 gratis – for nothing
1291 humorous – moody as his "humours" are imbalanced
1293 to be tickle a th' sear – to be easily triggered into laughter
1294 blank verse – verse that does not rhyme
1294 to halt – to stop, to prevent
1295 to be wont to do sth. – to be accustomed to doing sth.
1296 tragedian – tragic actors
1296 city – literally a city in Denmark, but for Shakespeare's audience it alludes to the city of London
1297 how chances it – for what reason
1299 inhibition – ban on performing plays, as was sometimes in effect in London
1300 innovation – recent political change
1301 estimation – reputation
1305 wonted – usual
1306 eyrie – nest
1306 eyas – young hawks
1306f that cry out on the top of question – child performers with their shrill voices dominate
1307 tyrannically – outrageously
1308 to berattle – to rattle, to overcome with noise
1308f common stages – public theatres
1309 rapier – a thin, light sword
1310 goose-quill – pens, i.e. playwrights

1312 to escot – to support, to pay

1312 quality – acting profession

1312f no longer than they can sing – until their voices break

1314 like – likely

1316 succession – their future profession as an adult

1317 to do – argument, debate

1318 to tar – to incite

1319 argument – new plays

1320 to go to cuffs – to quarrel

1320 question – the plot

1324 to carry it away – to win, to come out on top

1325f Hercules and his load – adds emphasis by referencing Hercules carrying the world

1328 to make mouths at s.o. – to mock s.o.

1329f picture in little – miniature portrait

1330 ’sblood – By God’s blood, used as a figure of speech

1334 appurtenance – fitting accompaniment

1335 to comply – to obey proper royal courtesy

1335 garb – appropriate way of behaving

1335 extent – the behaviour extended to the actors

1341 handsaw – Hamlet is only “mad” some of the time, otherwise he is well aware of what is going on around him.

1343 to hark – to ask someone to listen

1344f swaddling-clouts – swaddling clothes were wrapped around a newborn baby

1347 twice – old age was viewed as a kind of second childhood

1352 Roscius – Quintus Roscius Gallus (ca. 126 BC – 62 BC), a famous Roman actor

1355 buzz – dismissive phrase to interrupt Polonius

1359 history / pastoral – Polonius lists different genres of play

1360f scene individable – a play that cannot be classified

1361 poem unlimited – a universal play answering a general question

1361 Seneca – Seneca the Elder (54 BC–39 AD), Roman rhetorician and writer

1362 Plautus – Titus Maccius Plautus (254 BC–184 BC), Roman writer of comedies

1362 law of writ – laws of writing

1362 liberty – the freedom to break these laws

1363 only – best

1364 Jephthah – Biblical figure that killed his daughter to fulfill a promise to God

1369 passing – exceedingly

1374 follows not – is not the next line in the poem and is not logical

1377 lot – chance

1377 to wot – to know

1380 row – line

1380 chanson – song

1381 abridgement – something that cuts Hamlet short

1384 valanced – become fringed with a beard

1384 to beard – to defy, also more literally, to put a beard on Hamlet

1385 by’r lady – by Our Lady, referring to the Virgin Mary

1386 nearer to heaven – grown taller

1386f altitude – height

1387 chopine – wooden blocks placed under ladies shoes to make them taller

1387f uncurrent – not legal to use as currency

1388 cracked within the ring – broken, Hamlet is joking as in his time female roles were

played by men
1389 we'll e'en to't – we will go straight to it
1390 taste – sample
1391 quality – skill
1395 million – the crowd
1395 caviare – caviar, an expensive dish of fish eggs favoured by the elite
1395 general – general public
1396f whose judgements ... cried in the top of mine – whose opinions are worth more than mine
1397 digested – arranged
1398 modesty – restraint
1398 cunning – skill
1399 sallets – indecencies to suit less refined tastes
1400 savoury – highly flavoured
1400f to indict s.o. of sth. – to accuse s.o. of sth.
1401 affection – affectation
1402 fine – extravagance, splendour
1403 Aeneas' tale to Dido – in classical mythology, Dido falls in love with Aeneas after he recounts his experiences
1404 Priam – the king of Troy during the Trojan War
1407 rugged – harsh
1407 Pyrrhus – also known as Neoptolemus, son of warrior Achilles and princess Deidamia in Greek mythology
1407 th'Hyrcanian beast – the tiger of Hyrcania, known for its ferocity
1409 sable – black
1411 couched – hidden
1413 heradlry more dismal – blood
1414 total – entirely
1414 gules – red, a term taken from heraldry
1414 trick'd – adorned
1416 impasted – dried
1416 with the parching streets – the streets are hot with burning
1417 tyrannous – terrible, harsh
1419 o'ersized – oversized, covered
1419 coagulate – coagulated, refers to when a liquid becomes semi-solid; often used to describe blood
1419 gore – blood
1420 carbuncle – a red gem
1421 grandsire – grandfather
1424 discretion – judgement
1425 anon – shortly
1426 to strike too short at s.o. – to strike inadequately
1426 antique – old
1428 repugnant – resistant
1428 unequal match'd – unevenly matched
1430 whiff – the movement of the sword through the air
1430 fell – fierce, destructive
1431 unnerved – weakened
1431 senseless – without feeling
1431 Ilium – Troy, or specifically the royal palace there
1435 to decline – to fall
1435 milky – white due to old age
1437 painted – motionless, as if in a painting
1438 neutral – caught between two opposing factions
1438 matter – the effect of his will
1440 against – before
1441 rack – clouds
1442 orb – earth
1443 hush – silent
1444 to rend – to split, to rupture
1444 region – sky
1446 Cyclops – one-eyed giants in Greek mythology that helped make the gods' armour
1447 Mars – Roman god of war

1447 to forge – to create, usually refers to a metal object, heated and struck with a hammer
1447 proof – impenetrable
1447 eterne – forever
1448 remorse – pity
1450 out – get out
1451 synod – an assembly or group, usually of members of the clergy
1452 fellies – the outer part of a wheel
1452 wheel – wheel of fortune
1453 to bowl – to roll
1453 nave – central part of the wheel
1454 fiend – the fiends who reside in hell
1457 jig – a form of light entertainment that took place after the main play
1457 bawdry – obscene
1458 Hecuba – second wife of King Priam of Troy during the Trojan War
1459 to mobble – to muffle, to veil
1463 bisson – blinding
1463 rheum – tears
1464 for – instead of
1465 lank – feeble
1465 o'erteemed – exhausted by childbirth, Hecuba is said to have had at least 19 children
1465 loin – sexual organs
1467 to steep – to soak
1468 state – rule
1471 to mince – to chop
1474 milch – to produce tears, as if milking a cow
1475 passion – grief
1476 to turn one's colour – to become flush with grief
1479 to bestow s.o. – to lodge s.o.
1480 to use s.o. – to treat s.o.
1480 abstract – summaries
1481 chronicle – record
1481f you were better have – it would be better to have
1482 epitaph – a phrase written in memory of the dead, often inscribed on graves
1483 desert – worth
1484 God's bodkin – by God's little body, an exclamation of disbelief
1484 after – according to
1487 bounty – generosity
1490f The Murder of Gonzago – a fictional play
1493 for a need – if necessary
1493 to study – to memorise
1506 conceit – imagination
1507 to wan – to become pale
1508 distraction – distress
1508 aspect – face
1509 function – bodily actions
1514 cue – cause, also an acting term
1516 to cleave – to split
1517 to appal – to shock, to make pale
1517 free – innocent
1518 to confound – to confuse
1521 muddy-mettled – dull spirited, sluggish
1521 to peak – to mope
1522 John-a-dreams – a dreamy person
1522 unpregnant – unprompted by his cause, i.e. slow to deliver his father's revenge
1524 property – kingdom
1525 defeat – destruction
1526 pate – head
1528 to tweak – to pull
1528 to give s.o. the lie – to call s.o. a liar
1531 'swounds – by God's wounds, phrase used to show disbelief
1531f for it cannot be / But – for it cannot be anything else except
1532 to be pigeon-liver'd – to be lacking in courage

1532 gall – boldness
1534 kite – a bird of prey
1535 offal – intestines
1535 bawdy – indecent
1536 remorseless – pitiless
1536 kindless – lacking natural feeling
1541 drab – a prostitute
1542 scullion – a domestic servant
1543 about – be active, get to it
1547 malefaction – misdoing, crime
1552 to tent – to probe
1552 to the quick – upon the sensitive part
1552 to blench – to shrink or flinch
1557 spirits – referring to Hamlet's melancholy
1559 relative – relevant

ACT III, SCENE I
1561 conference – roundabout method
1563 to grate – to erode
1567 forward – ready
1568 crafty – cunning
1568 to keep aloof – to remain distant
1573 niggard – stingy, ungenerous
1574f to assay s.o. to sth. – to tempt s.o. to do sth.
1575 pastime – form of entertainment
1577 to overreach – to overtake, to pass
1586 edge – push, inclination
1591 to affront s.o. – to come face-to-face with s.o.
1592 espial – spies
1593 to bestow o.s. – to hide or position o.s.
1595 as he is behav'd – how he behaves
1600 wildness – madness
1603 gracious – addressed to the king, your grace
1605 exercise – religious practice, she is likely handed a prayer book
1610 smart – painful
1610 lash – whip
1611 harlot – whore
1611 to beauty – to make beautiful
1611 plast'ring art – cosmetics, make-up
1613 painted – superficial
1618 sling – catapult
1618 outrageous – excessive, cruel
1623 consummation – ending
1624 devoutly – expressing religious devotion
1625 rub – obstacle
1627 to shuffle sth. off – to remove or get rid of sth.
1627 coil – turmoil
1628 respect – consideration
1629 calamity – suffering
1630 scorn – insult
1631 contumely – insulting behaviour or language
1632 pang – pain
1632 to disprize – to undervalue, to dishonour
1632 law – legal system
1633 insolence – disrespect
1633 office – those in office, i.e. those in an elected position
1633 spurn – kick
1635 quietus – his release from debts, i.e. death
1636 bodkin – dagger
1636 fardel – burden
1637 to grunt – to groan
1639 bourn – boundary
1644 native hue – natural colour
1645 to sickly over – to make weak
1645 cast – shade
1646 pitch – character
1646 moment – impulse
1647 awry – away from the correct route

1649 nymph – in classical mythology, a minor female nature deity
1649 orison – prayer
1653 remembrance – tokens of love
1654 to redeliver – to give back
1663 honest – virtuous
1668 discourse – discussion
1669 commerce – interaction
1672 bawd – woman in charge of a brothel
1677 to inoculate – to cure
1677 stock – nature
1677 to relish of sth. – to retain sth.
1679 nunnery – a convent, also a slang term for a brothel
1680 indifferent – indifferently, fairly
1682 revengeful – vengeful
1682f at s.o.'s beck – at s.o.'s command
1691 plague – curse
1692 dowry – a transfer of property or money that is passed from the bride to her husband
1693 calumny – slander
1695 monster – if a man's wife was unfaithful, it was claimed he would grow horns
1698 paintings – use of make-up, cosmetics
1699 to jig – to dance
1700 to amble – to walk in an exaggerated manner
1700 to lisp – to speak with an affectation
1701 wantonness – innocence
1703 but one – except for one, referring to the king
1707 expectancy – hope
1708 glass – mirror
1708 mould of form – model for others
1710 deject – dejected
1714 unmatch'd – without equal
1714 blown – blooming
1718 spake – spoke
1720 to sit on brood – to brood over, to think deeply about something
1721 hatch – hatching
1721 disclose – disclosure
1724 to set sth. down – to decide sth.
1725 tribute – money paid by one country to another in exchange for peace
1727 variable – different
1727 to expel – to eject, to remove
1728 this something settled matter in his heart – the matter that he is focused on
1730 fashion of himself – his usual behaviour
1732 commencement – beginning
1738 round – blunt
1739 in the ear – within hearing distance
1740 to find s.o. – to discover s.o.'s secret

ACT III, SCENE II

1745 trippingly – nimbly, agile
1745 to mouth – to speak pompously
1746 I had as lief – I would have rather
1746 town-crier – someone employed to shout public announcements in the street
1748 torrent – outpouring
1748 tempest – violent storm
1749 to beget – to father
1749 temperance – moderation
1751 robustious – unruly, boisterous
1751 periwig-pated – wig-wearing
1752 groundling – member of the audience with the cheapest

tickets, standing near the front of the stage
1753 capable – able to understand
1753 dumb-show – mime
1754 to overdo – to perform in an excessive way
1754f Termagant – imaginary figure in old morality plays, often portrayed a violent character
1755 to out-Herod Herod – to be worse than King Herod, a violent figure from the New Testament
1758 tutor – guide
1759 observance – observation
1760 from – far from
1764 pressure – impression
1764 or come tardy off – performed badly
1765 unskilful – unsophisticated
1765 judicious – those with good judgement
1766 allowance – acknowledgement
1768f profanely – rudely, disrespectfully
1769 gait – way of walking
1770 pagan – someone with beliefs outside of the major world religions
1770 nor man – nor any man
1771 journeyman – apprentice
1772 abominably – unnaturally
1773 to reform – to correct, to improve
1775f there be of them – there be some amongst them
1776f to set s.o. on to do sth. – to encourage s.o. to do sth.
1777 barren – dull-witted, idiotic
1788 just – honourable
1789 to cope with s.o. – to bring into contact with s.o.
1791 advancement – preferment
1794 candied – sugared, i.e. flattering
1795 to crook – to bend
1795 pregnant – ready
1796 thrift – profit
1796 fawning – displaying exaggerated flattery
1799 to seal – to designate
1801 buffets – blows
1803 blood – passion
1803 commeddled – mixed together
1805 stop – note
1807 core – centre, also a pun on the Latin for heart, "cor"
1812 afoot – begun
1813 comment – serious consideration
1814 occulted – hidden
1815 to unkennel o.s. – to reveal o.s.
1818 Vulcan – Roman god of fire and blacksmiths
1818 stithy – forge
1818 heedful – careful
1819 to rivet – to fix upon
1823 theft – trickery
1824 idle – unoccupied
1826 How fares – Hamlet is asked how he is, but takes it to mean how he is eating.
1828 promise-crammed – full
1828 capon – a cockerel castrated to make its meat taste better
1835 to enact – to act
1838 brute – brutal, stupid
1838 part – role
1838 capital – important
1838 calf – fool
1840 to stay upon sth. – to wait for sth.
1840 patience – permission
1849 country – sexual, with a pun on the first syllable
1857 jig-maker – composer of jigs/dances
1859 within's – within these
1865 not thinking on – be forgotten
1865 hobby-horse – artificial

horse tied round someone's waist
b1867 protestation – solemn demonstration of love
b1867 to woo s.o. – to seek the affection of s.o.
1868 miching malicho – secret mischief
1869 belike – presumably
1870f to keep counsel – to keep a secret
1875 naught – indecent
1877 clemency – patience, leniency
1879 posy – short verse motto
1882 Phoebus – also known as Apollo, one of the most important deities in Greek and Roman mythology, god of sun, light, art, knowledge and more
1882 cart – chariot
1883 wash – the sea
1883 Tellus – also known as Terra Mater, Roman goddess of the earth
1883 orbed – round
1884 sheen – radiance
1886 Hymen – god of marriage
1887 commutual – mutually
1892 to distrust s.o. – to fear for s.o.
1893 to discomfort – to discourage
1894 to hold quantity – to keep in the same proportion
1895 in neither aught, or in extremity – either non-existent or excessive
1897 siz'd – quantified
1901 operant powers – active faculties
1901 to leave – to cease
1904 confound – damn
1906 accurst – cursed
1908 wormwood – a bitter plant, Hamlet suggests that the words sting bitterly
1916 validity – in reality
1918 mellow – ripe
1924 enacture – fulfilment
1926 on slender accident – as a result of the slightest incident
1927 aye – ever
1931 the great man down – the great man fallen
1932 advanc'd – having moved up in terms of status or wealth
1933 to tend on sth. – to serve sth.
1935 in want – being in need
1936 to season – to ripen
1939 device – plan
1946 anchor – a recluse or hermit
1946 cheer – joy
1946 scope – the best he can hope for
1947 opposite – opposing force
1947 to blank – to make pale
1949 here and hence – in this life and whatever comes next
1949 strife – conflict
1953 to beguile – to while away
1954 to rock – to gently move, as in rocking the cradle
1955 mischance – misfortune
1955 twain – two
1963 tropically – figuratively
1967 galled – guilty
1967 jade – horse
1967 to wince – to kick out in pain
1967 withers – part of the horse between the shoulder blades
1968 unwrung – free of discomfort
1970 chorus – a narrator-like role in the play
1972 to dally – to spend idle time together, perhaps suggesting sexual intercourse
1973 keen – quick, sharp
1976 to mis-take – to mistake in the usual sense and to take wrongly
1979 drug – poison
1979 agreeing – is right
1980 confederate – opportunity

1980 season – assist
1982 Hecate – the goddess of witchcraft in Greek mythology
1982 ban – curse
1983 dire – dreadful
1984 to usurp on sth. – to take sth. without right
1986 extant – still in existance
1986 choice – finest
1989 frighted – frightened
1989 false fire – a gun that fires a blank, i.e. fiction
1991 to give over sth. – to stop sth.
1994 strucken – wounded
1995 hart – male deer
1995 ungalled – uninjured
1996 to watch – to remain awake
1997 thus runs the world away – such is the way of the world
1998 feather – appropriate costume
1999 to turn Turk – to abandon
1999 Provincial – from Provence in France
1999 razed – cuts in the leather of the shoes
2000 fellowship – partnership
2000 cry – group
2003 Damon – a dear friend, alluding to Greek myth of Damon and Pythias
2004 to dismantle – to strip, to deprive
2005 Jove – also known as Jupiter, Roman god of sky and thunder and king of the gods
2006 pajock – peacock
2013 recorder – a woodwind instrument
2015 perdie – corruption of the French phrase "par dieu," meaning by God
2022 retirement – departure
2022 distempered – out of character
2024 choler – anger
2026 purgation – purging or cleaning, either spiritually or physically
2029 frame – order
2029 to start – to swerve, to avoid
2035 right breed – appropriate nature
2035 wholesome – sane
2045 amazement – alarm
2046 to stonish – to astonish
2047 sequel – consequence
2053 pickers – hands
2059 succession – the passing of the throne from one ruler to the next
2061 musty – stale
2063 to go about – to attempt
2063 to recover the wind – a hunting metaphor, suggesting that Hamlet is prey
2064 toil – net
2066 unmannerly – rude
2074 ventage – hole
2076 to discourse – to produce
2077 stop – hole
2083 sound me – question me
2083 compass – range
2084 organ – instrument
2087 to fret – to irritate, but also a pun on the frets found on musical instruments
2095 to be backed – to have the back
2098 by and by – at once
2102 witching time – when witchcraft takes place
2103 to yawn – to open
2104 contagion – infection
2106 to quake – to tremble
2108 Nero – Nero (37 AD–68 AD), Roman emperor who murdered his mother
2111 hypocrite – someone who pretends to have morals that he actually does not possess
2112 to shend o.s. – to reproach, verbally abuse

ACT III, SCENE III

2115 to let sth. range – to let sth. continue uncontrolled
2116 commission – command, instruction
2116 to dispatch – to make ready
2120 to provide o.s. – to prepare o.s.
2124 peculiar – private
2126 noyance – injury, harm
2127 weal – welfare
2128 cess – cessation, death
2129 gulf – whirlpool
2130 massy – massive, weighty
2133 to mortise – to attach securely
2133 to adjoin – to join
2134 annexment – accompaniment
2135 boist'rous – turbulent, violent
2137 to arm – to prepare
2138 fetter – restraint, chain
2141 to convey o.s. – to place o.s.
2142 process – proceedings
2142 to tax s.o. – to reprimand s.o.
2142 home – homely, bluntly
2145 partial – biased
2146 of vantage – a position of advantage
2150 primal – refers to God's curse on Cain for killing his brother Abel
2162 to forestall s.o. – to prevent s.o.
2165 to serve s.o.'s turn – to be of service in s.o.'s position
2167 effects – benefits
2169 th'offence – the profits from the offence
2171 to shove by sth. – to push sth. to one side
2173 to buy out sth. – to bribe sth.
2173 above – i.e. in heaven
2174 shuffling – evasion
2176 to the teeth and forehead of – to come face-to-face with
2177 to give in evidence – to submit evidence
2177 to rest – to remain
2181 limed – stuck in difficulty, as a bird trapped by lime, a sticky substance
2182 engag'd – trapped
2186 pat – conveniently
2188 that would be scann'd – that would be interpreted as follows
2192 hire and salary – something Hamlet might be paid for, as it would be to Claudius' benefit
2193 grossly – when enjoying life, i.e. full of sin
2194 broad blown – in full bloom
2195 audit – account
2199 passage – journey to the afterlife
2201 hent – opportunity
2205 relish – trace
2206 to trip s.o. – to send s.o. falling, i.e. to hell
2208 to stay – to await
2209 physic – medicine

ACT III, SCENE IV

2212 to lay home to s.o. – to speak plainly to s.o.
2213 prank – erratic behaviour
2213 broad – unrestrained
2214 to screen – to shield
2215 heat – Claudius' anger
2221 idle – frivolous, foolish
2224 by the rood – by the Christian cross
2244 too busy – too interfering
2245 to wring – to grab tightly
2248 to braze – to cover with brass
2249 proof – armoured
2249 bulwark – fortified
2249 sense – sensitivity, feeling
2250 to wag one's tongue – to speak so freely
2255 blister – a small, swollen blemish on the skin

2256 dicer – gambler
2257 contraction – a binding agreement, the marriage contract
2259 rhapsody – extravagance, meaningless
2260 mass – the earth
2263 index – table of contents prefacing a book
2265 counterfeit presentment – false representation
2267 front – face
2269 station – way of standing
2269 herald – messenger
2269 Mercury – winged messenger for the Roman gods
2270 new-lighted – newly alighted
2275 mildew'd – a disease affecting plants
2275 ear – an ear of corn
2278 to batten – to feed greedily
2278 moor – marshland, but also suggesting a dark-skinned person to contrast with the "fair mountain"
2280 heyday – youthful period of passion
2281 judgment – reason
2284 apoplex'd – having lost bodily function
2285 thrall'd – enthralled
2288 to cozen – to cheat
2288 hoodman-blind – a game now called blindman's bluff, Hamlet suggests Gertrude must have been blindfolded to make such a bad choice
2290 sans – without
2292 to mope – to act dull or stupid
2294 to mutine – to mutiny
2297 compulsive – compelling, irrepressible
2297 ardour – passion
2297 to give the charge – to attack
2298 frost – age
2299 to pander – to give way to
2301 grained – engrained
2302 tinct – colour
2303 enseamed – saturated with grease
2304 to stew – to be soaked
2304 to honey – to exchange affectionate remarks
2305 sty – an enclosure for pigs
2308 tithe – tenth part
2309 precedent – previous
2309 vice – embodiment of wickednesss
2310 cutpurse – pickpocket
2318 to chide – to scold, to disapprove of
2319 laps'd in time and passion – lets time pass and passion fade
2320 important – urgent
2320 acting – carrying out
2322 to whet – to sharpen, to stimulate
2325 conceit – imagination
2328 vacancy – vacant or empty space
2329 incorporal – insubstantial
2332 bedded – laying flat
2332 like life in excrements – as if it had a life of its own
2337 conjoin'd – joined together
2338 capable – respond
2340 stern – grim, vengeful
2341 colour – character
2341 for – in place of
2348 habit – clothing or demeanour
2348 as he liv'd – as when he was alive
2349 portal – door
2350 coinage – invention
2353 temperately – in time
2356 to re-word – to repeat
2357 to gambol from sth. – to wander away from sth.
2358 unction – ointment
2359 trespass – sin
2360 to skin – to form a skin over sth.

2360 ulcerous – infected, corrupted
2361 to mine – to undermine, to corrode
2366 fatness – indulgence
2366 pursy – short-winded with over-indulgence
2368 to curb – to bow
2368 to woo for sth. – to entreat, to request
2374 to eat – to consume
2377 frock – a gown or dress
2377 livery – uniform
2378 to refrain – to abstain, i.e. from sleeping with Claudius
2381 use – habit
2383 potency – power
2388 their – heaven's
2388 scourge and minister – agent of revenge
2389 to bestow – to dispose of
2389 to answer sth. – to justify or pay for sth.
2392 this bad begins – this has begun badly
2392 to remain behind – to follow
2395 bloat – bloated
2396 wanton – unrestrained
2397 reechy – filthy
2398 to paddle – to play with gently
2399 to ravel sth. out – to unravel or find sth. out
2401 in craft – by design, deliberately
2403 paddock – toad
2403 gib – male cat
2404 concerning – matter
2406 to unpeg – to unfasten
2407 ape – presumably refers to a now-forgotten story of an ape that broke its neck trying to imitate the birds
2408 to try conclusions – to experiment
2414 to conclude on sth. – to be decided
2416 adder – a poisonous snake
2418 to marshal – to lead
2418 knavery – mischief
2419 enginer – engineer
2420 to hoist – to lift
2420 petard – a war engine filled with explosive materials
2420f and't shall go hard / But I – and the difficulty must be great if I cannot
2424 to pack – to hurry
2425 to lug – to drag
2429 to draw toward an end with you – to finish dealings with you

ACT IV, SCENE I

2431 matter – meaning
2431 heave – breathing with great effort
2434 to bestow this place on s.o. – to let s.o. have privacy
2437 to contend – to struggle in rivalry
2438 fit – rage
2441 brainish – deranged
2441 apprehension – understanding
2442 heavy – sorrowful
2443 It had been so with us had we been there – It would have happended to Claudius had he been there
2447 to lay sth. to s.o. – to lay the blame on s.o.
2447 providence – foresight
2448 out of haunt – away from others
2452 to divulge – to become apparent
2455 ore – precious metal
2456 mineral – mine
2460 to ship – to send away by ship
2462 to countenance – to explain
2463 some further aid – assistance
2466 fair – gently
2470 untimely – prematurely, i.e. Polonius' death

2472 blank – target
2475 discord – disagreement

ACT IV, SCENE II

2476 to stow – to put something away; Hamlet is referring to Polonius' body
2480 to compound – to mix, to combine
2486 to demand of s.o. – to question s.o.
2486 replication – response
2489 countenance – favour
2490 authority – power or influence
2492 to mouth – to take in the mouth

ACT IV, SCENE III

2504 strong – strict
2505 distracted – weak-brained, confused
2506 in – by
2507 scourge – punishment
2508 to bear all smooth and even – to manage matters smoothly
2510 deliberate – carefully considered
2511 appliance – remedy
2520f convocation – assembly
2521 politic – political, discerning
2521 e'en – even now
2522 diet – pun on the Diet of Worms, a political assembly in 16th century Germany
2524 service – dishes, meals
2531 progress – alludes to the royal progress or journey of state
2534 i'th'other place – i.e. in hell
2535 to nose – to smell
2540 to tender sth. – to hold sth. dear
2542 fiery – intense
2543 bark – ship
2544 th'associates – the companions on the journey
2550 cherub – a type of angel known for being insightful
2558 to lean on sth. – to depend on sth.
2559 England – the king of England
2559 at aught – any worth
2561 cicatrice – scar
2563f thou mayst not coldly set / Our sovereign process – you may not disregard our royal order
2564 at full – fully
2565 congruing to that effect – concerning that matter
2567 hectic – fever
2569 hap – fortune

ACT IV, SCENE IV

2572 to crave – to want
2572 conveyance – movement from one place to another
2572 to promise – to have previously agreed
2573 rendezvous – appointed meeting place
2577 softly – carefully
2578 powers – troops
2580 How purpos'd – what is their purpose
2584 main – centre
2585 frontier – outlying land
2587 patch – portion
2589 to pay five ducats – to pay five gold coins
2591 rank – high
2593 to garrison – to station troops
2595 straw – insignificant matter
2596 impostume – abscess, a pus-filled inflamation
2601 occasion – event
2601 to inform against s.o. – to act against his irresolution
2602 to spur – to urge
2603 market of his time – the sale or use of his time
2605 discourse – comprehension

2608 to fust – to grow fusty or mouldy
2609 bestial – animal-like
2609 oblivion – mindlessness
2609 craven – cowardly
2609 scruple – hesitation
2610 on – about
2613 this thing's to do – this act is yet to be done
2615 gross – plain
2615 to exhort – to urge
2616 charge – cost
2617 delicate – raised in luxury
2619 invisible – possible
2622f Rightly to be great / Is not to stir without great argument – to be great means not fighting over something insignificant
2624 but greatly to find quarrel – but to fight when honour is at risk
2627 excitement – impetus
2630 for a fantasy and trick of fame – for the illusion of fame won in battle
2631 plot – piece of land
2633 continent – something that contains. Hamlet argues that the land is not even big enough to bury all the soldiers.

ACT IV, SCENE V

2636 importunate – insistent
2637 distract – agitated
2640 to hem – to hesitate in speaking
2641 to spurn at sth. – to react angrily at sth.
2641 enviously – impatiently
2641 things in doubt – things of unclear meaning
2644 to collection – to draw conclusions, to attempt to find meaning
2644 to aim at sth. – to guess at sth.
2645 to botch sth. up – to stitch sth. up messily
2646 to yield – to convey
2646 them – to them
2647f there might be thought, / Though nothing sure, yet much unhappily – there might be something intended, though nothing is clear except that it is an unhappy message
2649 to strew – to spread
2650 conjecture – speculation
2650 ill-breeding – mischief-making
2653 toy – trifle
2653 amiss – calamity
2654 artless – clumsy
2655 to spill o.s. – to be excessive
2660 cockle – cockleshell, worn by pilgrim visitors to the Spanish shrine of Santiago of Compostela
2661 shoon – shoes
2663 Say you? – What is it you say?
2666 turf – piece of grass
2667 stone – gravestone
2671 shroud – clothes worn in the grave
2673 to lard – to cover
2677 good dild you – God yield you, i.e. give you what you deserve
2684 betime – early
2686 Valentine – sweetheart
2687 to don – to put on
2688 to dup – to open
2693 Gis – Jesus
2693 Charity – a saint in the Catholic Church
2695 if they come to't – if they have a chance
2696 Cock – euphemism for God, but also suggesting penis
2697 to tumble – to have sex with
2703f I cannot choose but weep – I can only weep

2712 spy – scouts sent ahead of an army
2713 battalion – large military unit
2714 author – cause
2715 remove – removal
2715 muddied – stirred up
2716 thick – confused
2717 for – because of
2718 in hugger-mugger – in secrecy
2723 wonder – bewilderment
2723 in clouds – in a state of suspicion or confusion
2724 buzzer – gossip, rumours
2726 necessity – driven by necessity to find the cause of his father's death
2726 of matter beggar'd – deprived of solid facts
2727 to stick – to accuse
2727 to arraign s.o. – to call before a court
2729 murd'ring-piece – a small canon that discharged its shot widely and so could kill more people
2731 Switzers – Swiss guards, often employed to protect royal households
2733 overpeering of his list – rising over its boundary
2734 flats – flat or low-lying land
2734 impetuous – hasty, impulsive
2735 head – rebellion, insurrection
2736 to overbear – to overpower
2736 rabble – unruly group
2737 as – as if
2738 antiquity – ancient traditions
2739 ratifier – approvers, those with the capacity to confirm something formally
2739 prop – support
2744 counter – a hunting term suggesting they are following the wrong scent, i.e. going in the wrong direction
2752 cuckold – a man whose wife had been unfaithful
2752 to brand s.o. – to make a mark on s.o. usually by burning
2753 unsmirched – unstained, pure
2754 true – faithful
2756 fear our person – fear for our person
2757 to hedge – to protect
2758 to peep – to catch a glimpse
2758 to – at
2758 what it would – what it would like to do
2760 incens'd – angered
2763 to demand one's fill – to make one's demands in full
2764 to juggle – to deceive, to trick
2766 grace – religious feeling
2766 pit – hell
2767 to dare sth. – to be willing to risk
2768 both the worlds – this life and beyond
2770 throughly – thoroughly, completely
2770 to stay s.o. – to prevent s.o.
2771 not all the world's – not the entire world's
2772 to husband sth. – to manage sth.
2776 swoopstake – indiscriminately
2776 to draw – to gather
2780 life-rend'ring pelican – the pelican was believed to feed its young with its own blood
2781 to repast – to feed
2784 most sensibly – most feeling
2785 level – directly
2788 salt – salty
2789 virtue – power
2791 to turn – to tilt

2791 beam – bar of the scales
2795 fine in – refined by
2796 instance – token or sign
2798 bier – a movable stand used to carry the corpse to the grave
2803 a-down a-down – a well-known song
2804 wheel – refrain
2805 steward – character in the ballad
2807 rosemary – a herb symbolising remembrance
2808 pansy – a flower symbolising love
2809 document – lesson
2811 fennel – vegetable symbolising flattery
2811 columbine – flowers symbolising infidelity
2811 rue – herb symbolising repentence
2813 difference – a variation on a coat of arms, but also implying that Gertrude must wear it differently
2814 daisy – flower perhaps symbolising deception
2816 bonny – pleasing, sweet
2817 passion – extreme grief
2818 favour – charm
2825 flaxen – white
2825 poll – head
2827 moan – lament
2831 to commune with sth. – to share sth.
2833 of whom your wisest friends you will – choose your wisest friends
2834 'twixt – between
2835 collateral – indirect
2836 touch'd – implicated
2842 his means of death – the way that he died
2842 obscure – secret
2843 trophy – memorial
2843 hatchment – tablet placed over the tomb with the deceased's coat of arms
2844 ostentation – ceremony
2846 to call sth. in question – to demand an explanation

ACT IV, SCENE VI
2857 ambassador – a diplomatic official
2859f to overlook – to look over, to read
2860 means – means of access
2862 appointment – equipment
2863 grapple – boarding process
2864 to board – to go on board a ship
2865f of mercy – merciful
2866 to do a turn – to do s.o. a favour
2867 to repair – to come
2870 bore – the inside of the barrel of a gun; Hamlet suggests his words are bullets.

ACT IV, SCENE VII
2878 acquittance – innocence
2879 for – as a
2880 knowing – understanding
2883 to proceed against sth. – to take action against sth.
2883 feat – events, crimes
2884 capital – punishable by death
2886 to stir s.o. up – to be prompted to do sth.
2887 unsinew'd – weak
2889 look – at the sight (of Hamlet)
2890 be it either which – be it either or
2891 conjunctive – closely connected
2894 count – account
2894 might – can
2895 the general gender – the common people
2898 grace – virtue
2899 slightly – lightly
2899 to timber – to create with wood

2900 to revert – to return
2904 if praises may go back again – if praises may recall how Ophelia used to be
2907 to break – to interrupt
2908 flat – lacking in spirit
2909 shook with danger – threatened
2919 high and mighty – the king
2919 naked – destitute
2924 should – does
2925 abuse – deceit
2926 character – handwriting
2938 to check – to cancel, to deviate
2939 to work s.o. to sth. – to persuade s.o. to sth.
2940 exploit – task
2940 device – devising
2943 to uncharge sth. – to deem sth. blameless
2943 practice – plot
2946 organ – the instrument or cause
2948 in Hamlet's hearing – within earshot of Hamlet
2949 parts – talents
2952 siege – lowest rank
2953 ribbon – a thin strip of material
2955 livery – uniform
2956 weeds – garments
2957 graveness – seriousness
2960 gallant – fine, young man
2963 as – as if
2963f to be incorpsed with sth. – to be in one body with sth.
2963f to be demi-natured with sth. – to be half of the same nature with sth.
2964 to top – to surpass
2965 forgery – imagining
2966 to come short of sth. – to be inferior to sth.
2968 Lamord – similar to "la mort", meaning "death" in French, adding a sense of foreboding
2969 brooch – jewel
2971 to make confession of s.o. – to make report of s.o.'s skill
2973 defence – self-defence
2976 scrimer – fencer
2977 motion – movement
2977 guard – defence
2977 eye – vision
2979 to envenom – to become bitter
2981 to play – to compete
2988 passages of proof – events that have proven it
2989 to qualify – to diminish
2991 wick – a piece of material that is lit for a candle or lamp
2991 snuff – portion of the wick that no longer provides light
2991 to abate – to reduce
2993 pleurisy – inflammation or swelling
2996 abatement – delay
2998 spendthrift – wasteful, extravagant
2999 quick – most sensitive point
2999 ulcer – a sore on the skin
3003 to sanctuarize – to offer protection against
3007 to put s.o. on – to encourage s.o. to do sth.
3008 varnish – a coating often applied to wood to give it a glossy, shiny outer layer
3010 to wager over sth. – to bet on who will win
3010 remiss – careless
3011 contriving – plotting
3012 to peruse – to examine
3014 unbated – not blunted
3015 to requite s.o. – to repay s.o.
3016 to anoint – to rub with liquid
3017 mountebank – quack doctor
3019 cataplasm – plaster, cure
3020 simples – medicinal herbs
3023 contagion – poison
3023 to gall – to graze

3025 weigh what convenience – consider
3026 shape – purpose
3027 to look through sth. – to become visible
3028 to essay – to attempt
3029 back – back-up
3029 second – secondary option
3030 to blast – to fail
3030 proof – testing
3033 dry – dry-mouthed
3034 as – you should
3034 bout – round in a fight
3036 chalice – drinking cup
3036 for the nonce – for the purpose
3036 to sip – to drink a small amount of sth.
3037 venom'd – poisoned
3037 stuck – thrust
3042 askant – across
3043 hoary – greyish-white
3043 glassy – clear
3044 fantastic – fanciful
3045 crow-flower – a type of wild flower
3045 nettle – a stinging plant
3045 long purple – a type of purple orchid
3046 liberal – unrestrained
3046 gross – vulgar
3048 pendent – overhanging
3048 crownet – small crown
3049 to clamber – to climb with difficulty
3049 sliver – branch
3050 weedy – made of wild flowers
3053 which time – during which time
3053 snatch – small part
3053 laud – a song or hymn
3054 incapable – unaware
3055f indued unto sth. – adapted to sth.
3058 lay – song
3063 trick – habit
3064 these – his tears
3065 the woman – the woman in Laertes, his feminine side
3067 to dout sth. – to extinguish sth.

ACT V, SCENE I

3072 wilfully – deliberately, referring to Ophelia's suicide
3074 straight – straight away, immediately
3074 crowner – coroner
3079 se offendendo – Latin for "in self-offence"
3080 wittingly – knowingly
3081 branch – part
3082 argal – corruption of Latin ergo, meaning "therefore"
3083 Goodman – title below gentleman and often followed by the individual's occupation
3084 Delver – digger
3087 will he nill he – whether it is his intention or not
3092 quest – inquest
3094 gentlewoman – woman of high social standing
3098 even-Christen – fellow Christians
3099 ditcher – ditch maker
3100 to hold up – to continue
3102 arms – a coat of arms, but also literally meaning limbs as Adam was the first man
3105 the Scripture – the Bible
3107 confess thyself – a saying that continues: "confess thyself and be hanged"
3111 gallows-maker – a gallows is a wooden frame used to hang people
3119 to unyoke – to give up
3123 to cudgel – to beat
3124 to mend one's pace – to improve one's speed
3127 stoup – tankard
3130 to contract – to pass
3130 o / a – noises that the grave-

digger makes as he carries out his work
3130 behove – duty
3134 easiness – indifference
3136 dainty – sensitive
3138 to claw – to grab
3138 clutch – claws
3142 to jowl – to throw, to strike
3143f politician – schemer
3144 to circumvent – to outwit
3149 such-a-one – of an unspecified name
3150 to beg – to borrow
3152 chopless – jaw-less
3153 mazard – head
3154 revolution – change of fortune
3155 loggets – a game where wooden pins are thrown around
3158 shrouding-sheet – a sheet that is wrapped around a corpse
3162 quiddity / quillity – distinctions, verbal subtleties
3163 tenure – property documents
3163f to suffer s.o. to do sth. – to allow s.o. to do sth.
3164 sconce – head
3165 action of battery – legal term for physical assault
3166 statute – legal document similar to a mortgage
3166 recognizance – legal document relating to debt
3167 voucher – people who vouch for s.o.'s ownership of land
3167 recovery – along with fines, part of a legal process to secure land ownership
3170f a pair of indentures – two copies of a legal agreement
3171 conveyance – deed relating to the transfer of land
3172 box – coffin
3172 inheritor – owner
3174 jot – smallest part
3175 parchment – material to be written upon
3177 assurance – security
3178 sirrah – sir, generally used when speaking to inferiors
3183 lie – the clown begins punning on the sense of lying down and to be untruthful
3185 quick – living
3195 absolute – precise
3195 by the card – literally
3196 equivocation – ambiguity
3196 to undo – to get the better of
3197 picked – smart
3199 kibe – chilblain, a sore on the hands or feet caused by the cold
3221 pocky – diseased
3221 to hold – to hold together
3221f laying in – being lain in the ground
3222 tanner – someone who turns animal skin into leather by tanning
3225 hide – skin
3227 of your whoreson dead body – wretched
3228 lien – lain
3234 flagon – large container of liquid
3239 jest – laughter, playfulness
3240 abhorred – filled with horror
3241 my gorge rises – the contents of my stomach rise
3242 gibe – taunts
3242 gambol – frolic
3243f to set s.o. on a roar – to cause s.o. to roar with laughter
3245 chop-fallen – downcast
3246 favour – appearance
3249 Alexander – Alexander III of Macedon, known as Alexander the Great, king of Macedon and military leader
3256 to stop – to plug

3256 bung-hole – hole in a barrel
3257 too curiously – too closely
3261 loam – mixture of clay and sand
3263 imperious – imperial
3265 earth – earth made from some great individual's body
3266 to expel – to keep out
3266 flaw – gust of wind
3269 maimed – shortened, incomplete
3269 to betoken – to indicate
3271 estate – status
3277 warranty – authority
3278 that great command – the king's orders
3278 to oversway – to overrule
3278 order – usual custom
3279 should – should have been
3279 unsanctified – unholy, i.e. land outside the church grounds
3280 the last trumpet – judgement day
3280 for – instead of
3281 shards, flints, and pebbles – fragments of pottery and small stones
3283 maiden – girl or young married woman
3283 strewments – flowers
3286 to profane – to make unholy
3289 unpolluted – pure
3290 churlish – rude, stingy
3291 to minister – to authorise religious worship
3292 when thou liest howling – when you are in hell
3295 to deck – to cover with flowers
3298 ingenious – intelligent
3303 Pelion – a mountain in Thessaly, Greece
3303 skyish – reaching the sky
3304 Olympus – the mountain where the Greek gods lived
3305 emphasis – strength of expression
3307 wonder-wounded – paralysed by wonder
b3309 to grapple with s.o. – to fight with s.o.
3311 splenative – hot-headed
3314 asunder – apart
3325 to forbear s.o. – to leave s.o. alone
3326 thou't – you shall
3327 woo't – will you
3328 eisel – vinegar
3330 to outface s.o. – to outdo s.o.
3332 to prate – to rant
3334 to singe – to burn
3334 the burning zone – the sun's orbit
3335 Ossa – another mountain in Thessaly, Greece
3335 wart – small, hard blemish on the skin
3335 to mouth – to talk
3339 couplets – small pair of birds
3339 disclos'd – hatched
3340 to droop – to hang down
3344 to mew – to make a sound like a cat
3344 and dog will have his day – phrase meaning every person's time will come
3346 in – by remembering
3347 push – test
3349 monument – suggests that Hamlet's death by Laertes will be a fitting memorial for Ophelia's death

ACT V, SCENE II

3357 mutine – mutineer
3357 bilboes – chains
3358 rashness – impulsiveness
3359 indiscretion – lack of long-term planning
3360 do pall – do fail
3361 end – outcome

3362 to rough-hew sth. – to carve sth. roughly
3364 sea-gown – short-sleeved gown often worn by sailors
3364 to scarf – to wrap loosely
3365 to grope – to feel with one's hands
3365 them – Hamlet is referring to Rosencrantz and Guildenstern
3365 had my desire – find what I was looking for
3366 to finger – to steal
3371 to lard – to garnish
3372 importing – concerning
3373 bug – terror
3374 supervise – reading (of the royal letter)
3374 to bate – to wait
3375 to stay sth. – to wait for sth.
3380 benetted – surrounded
3383 fair – in elegant handwriting
3384 statist – statesman
3385 baseness – a mark of lowly status
3387 yeoman's service – efficient
3389 earnest – serious
3389 conjuration – entreaty, request
3390 tributary – country owing money to another
3392 wheaten – made of wheat, a symbol of peace
3393 comma – punctuation mark indicating a small break, here suggesting a closeness between Denmark and England
3393 amity – friendship
3394 "as"es – phrases beginning with "as"
3394 charge – importance
3398 shriving-time – time for confession and repentance
3399 to be ordinant – to be in control
3400 signet – seal
3401 model – identical copy
3402 writ – mandate, command
3403 to subscribe – to sign
3403 impression – seal
3404 changeling – substitution
3405 to be sequent – to follow
3407 to go to it – to go to death
3408 to make love to sth. – to court sth.; Hamlet suggests Rosencrantz and Guildenstern brought their fate upon themselves
3410 insinuation – behaviour
3412 fell – fierce
3413 opposite – opponents
3414 Does it not … stand me now upon – is it not imperative that I do this?
3415 to whore s.o. – to make a whore of s.o.
3416 to pop in – to intercept
3416 election – the designation of the monarch
3417 angle – fishing hook
3418 coz'nage – deception
3419 to quit s.o. – to repay s.o.
3420 canker – an ulcer or sore
3421 in – to
3424 interim – short period of time
3429 portraiture – representation
3430 bravery – extravagant display
3433 waterfly – a type of insect
3436 beast – animal
3437 crib – place that an animal eats from
3437 mess – table
3437 chuff – either a chattering bird or an ill-mannered individual
3438 spacious – plentiful
3441 diligence – effort
3442 bonnet – type of hat
3446 sultry – oppressively hot
3446f complexion – temperament
3450 wager – bet
3455 newly – recently
3456 excellent differences – different excellences

3457 showing – outward appearance
3457 feelingly – openly
3458 continent – entirety
3460 definement – description
3460 perdition – destruction
3461 inventorially – as a list
3461 to dozy – to make dizzy
3462 to yaw – to lag behind
3462 neither – and nothing else
3462 in respect of – in relation to
3463 verity – truth
3463 extolment – high praise
3463f of great article – of great importance
3464 infusion – possessing
3464 dearth – scarcity
3465 diction – speech
3465 semblable – semblance, likeness
3466 umbrage – shadow, pale imitation
3467 infallibly – correctly
3468 concernancy – reason for this talk
3469 raw – inadequate
3480 to approve s.o. – to compliment s.o.
3484 imputation – attribute
3485 by them – by those that have seen his fencing
3485 meed – merit
3485 to be unfellowed – to have no equal
3489 Barbary horse – highly valued North African horses
3490 to impawn – to wager
3491 poniard – dagger
3491 assign – accessories
3491 girdle – sword belt
3491 hanger – loops from which swords are hung
3492 carriage – another word for hanger
3492 fancy – artistic in appearance
3492 responsive – well-matched
3493 liberal – elaborate
3493 conceit – design
3495 to edify – to instruct
3495 margin – explanation, often included in a book's margin
3496 to have done – to be finished
3498 german – relevant
3503 to lay – to wager
3503f that in a dozen passes … he shall not exceed you three hits – that in 12 rounds, Laertes' number of hits will not exceed Hamlet's by three or more
3505 trial – test
3506 vouchsafe the answer – accept the challenge
3510 breathing time of day – time when exercise takes place
3514 deliver – report
3515 after what – according to
3519 for's turn – to do it for him
3520 lapwing – bird symbolising hurry, as it was known for leaving the nest as soon as it was hatched
3521 dug – breast; Horatio implies that Osric would have complimented his mother's breast before sucking it
3522 drossy – worthless
3523 to dote on sth. – to praise sth. excessively
3524 yeasty – frothy, excessive
3524 collection – collection of words and mannerisms
3525 fanned – spread out
3525 winnowed – selective
3526 bubble – they burst easily like bubbles
3529 to hold – to remain, to continue
3532 if his fitness speaks – if the time is right
3536 entertainment – good-natured conversation
3541 odds – the odds given by Claudius

3544 gaingiving – misgiving, foreboding
3546f to forestall sth. – to delay sth.
3547 repair – coming
3548 not a whit – not at all
3548 to defy – to refuse to believe
3548 augury – prophecy
3549 it – his death
3552 betimes – early
3556 this presence – this royal assembly
3559 exception – objection
3566 faction – group
3569 disclaiming – denial
3578 ungor'd – uninjured
3584 foil – sword used in fencing
3586 to stick off – to stand out
3592 to be bettered – to be considered better
3594 a – the same
3598 or quit in answer of the third exchange – or reply in the third exchange by hitting Laertes
3599 battlement – top of a wall, usually around a castle, used to shoot from
3601 union – valuable pearl
3604 kettle – kettle-drum
3605 cannoneer – person who fires a cannon
3608 wary – careful
3614 palpable – plainly seen, obvious
3622 fat – sweaty, overweight
3623 napkin – handkerchief
3624 to carouse to sth. – to make a toast to sth.
3634 to pass – to thrust
3635 wanton – spoilt child
b3639 to scuffle – to fight closely
3646 to swoon – to faint
3663 potion – drink
3663 union – pearl
3664 to serve s.o. justly – to give s.o. what they deserve
3665 to temper – to mix
3671 chance – event
3673 sergeant – i.e. death
3682 shall I leave behind me – shall follow after my death
3684 felicity – happiness, i.e. of heaven
3689 volley – firing of weapons
3690 to overcrow sth. – to triumph over sth.
3692f to light on s.o. – the selection of the next Danish king
3694 occurent – event
3694 more and less – great and small
3695 to solicit – to prompt
b3699 colours – banners
3701 quarry – pile of the dead
3701 to cry on sth. – to suggest sth.
3702 cell – dwelling
3703 a – one
3706 the ears – Claudius' ears
3718 carnal – passionate, referring to Claudius and Gertrude's marriage
3719 judgment – punishment
3719 casual – occurring by chance
3720 to put sth. on – to arrange sth.
3721 upshot – conclusion
3726 rights of memory – old rights
3727 vantage – advantage
3734 to put s.o. on – to put s.o. to the test as king
3739 field – battlefield
f peal of ordnance – firing of cannons